WHAT PEOPLE ARE SAYING ABOUT

DYING TO BE FREE

This is one book you won't want to miss! *Dying to Be Free* is an exceptionally beautiful and well-written book. Hannah Robinson's near-death experience is dramatic. Her well-documented interactions with her father, a Catholic priest, has lessons of forgiveness for us all. The powerful insights and understandings in this highly recommended book could change your life.

Lee Jeffrey Long, MD, author of *The New York Times* bestselling *Evidence of the Afterlife: The Science of Near-Death Experiences*

Hannah Robinson paints a view of the near-death experience like the thousands of others currently on the market. She shows what it is like to be the daughter of a Catholic Priest, her mother continuously turned down by cardinals and parish priests when asked for advice on how best to handle 'the situation'. Young Hannah's longing to be loved by her father pushed her into a hedonistic lifestyle that climaxed when she ran off – ignoring cars and road hazards. From the blackness of a terrible fall, she woke in light... an unbelievable, incredible, awe-inspiring everywhere light. Yet her body far below was surrounded by medics, an ambulance, and a flurry of activity in a rush to get her to a hospital. She felt both exhilarated and joyfilled, without pain and surgeries came later. What remained was the otherness of what had just happened to her.

One of the strengths of this book is the clarity she gained in coming to terms with the difference between the love she experienced 'over there' and the despair she still had to deal with here. No matter how wondrous a near-death experience, it does not save you from having to face your problems. With a new consciousness, she discovered the power of forgiveness... a mixed...

PMH Atwater, LHD, One of the o

D1328692

near-death studies. Among her books are: *The Big Book of Near-Death Experiences*

Hannah Robinson's life journey – from her near-fatal accident, to her resulting near-death experience – took her on a spiritual quest to understand the deepest meaning of those events. Her book is a well-written, well-documented testimony to living a life where self-creation, through love, is the greatest power. I thank you, Hannah, for sharing your story.

Dannion Brinkley, NDE Survivor, *New York Times* bestselling author of *Saved by the Light* and *Secrets of the Light*

Hannah Robinson, the author of this work, is the forbidden fruit of impossible love which unites a woman to a Catholic priest. Her narrative of NDE shows us to what extent this experience can determine to make us understand that Love is over everything. Her story which is read as a novel is as moving as it is fascinating.

Jean Jacques Charbonier, MD, award-winning international speaker and author of *7 Reasons to Believe in the Afterlife*, Inner Traditions: Rochester, Vermont

Hannah Robinson has quite a story to tell, and a storyteller's gift. She speaks of a unique journey – sired by a father who was a Father (a Catholic Priest), yet not quite her father – and undergoing a grisly 'death' that was not quite a death, but her birth into new light and life. For those interested in Near-Death Experiences – and full-bodied experiences of struggle and healing – you will find in Hannah Robinson a sympathetic soul.

Drew Leder, MD, PhD, Loyola University of Maryland, author of *The Absent Body, Spiritual Passages* and *Sparks of the Divine: Finding Inspiration in Our Everyday World*

Hannah Robinson bares her mind and soul in this heartfelt book, *Dying to Be Free*. Hannah's NDE signifies an amazing gift from God that led to personal change. Within the heart of this book beats a steady theme – personal transformation based on divine connection. Not only did Hannah begin to view herself through the divine eyes of love, she began to see her relationships from a perspective of unconditional regard. This was especially true regarding her estranged father. Because of this life re-frame, Hannah mended her broken heart by discovering forgiveness and peace. Personally, I was moved by this personal account of deep change through divine spirit and I have no doubt that many readers will share this sentiment.

Roy L. Hill, PsyD, author of *Psychology and the Near Death Experience: Searching for God*

Dying to Be Free is an astutely written autobiographical novel which captivates the reader from the first pages... (Hannah Robinson's) vivid narration of NDE is perfectly coupled with a powerful journey towards spirituality... The book is a lighthouse in the dark clouded sea, reminding us that nothing is predefined for any of us. The book is an excellent paradigm of Joseph Campbell's words; none of us lives the life that we intended. The author vividly reminds us that our life's path is revealed to us through errors, challenges, pain and only if we allow ourselves to undertake and embrace such a quest will we be able to see and experience it. This is an inspirational book.

Nikolaos Souvlakis, MBACP Accred & Reg, MBPsS, IAFP, Researcher of Spirituality and Psychotropic Disorders, Psychologist, Psychotherapist

A gripping account of the author's courageous struggles with her identity, the Catholic Church and a near-death experience. Hannah's story has a healing message of love, hope and peace regarding what lies ahead of us all.

Anna Lubelska, Director of Spiritual England and Coordinator of the Peaceful Schools Movement

Bravely challenging the accepted secrecy over children of priests, the author shares her personal struggle of identity and the Near-Death Experience that ultimately saves her life.

Tracy Goza, PhD, author of *I Heart Heaven: A Psychotherapist's Biblical Validation for Near-Death Experiences*

Hannah Robinson has written a truly moving narrative which encompasses the arc of her life and her search for answers... Hannah guides us from her initial rejection of organized religion to her realization of a higher spiritual directive which, unbeknownst to many of us, intersects all of our lives. Hannah illustrates that by examining the trials we suffer through and researching the experiences of others we can come to a rational comprehension of a Divine Spirituality... Hannah's experience is the epitome of the saying that truth can set you free.

Brian Foster, Spiritist blog at nwspiritism.com, author of *What Really Happens During Near Death Experiences, According to Spiritism*

Dying to Be Free

From Enforced Secrecy to Near Death to True Transformation

Dying to Be Free

From Enforced Secrecy to Near Death to True Transformation

Hannah Robinson

BOOKS

Winchester, UK
Washington, USA

First published by O-Books, 2016
O-Books is an imprint of John Hunt Publishing Ltd., Laurel House, Station Approach,
Alresford, Hants, SO24 9JH, UK
office1@jhpbooks.net
www.johnhuntpublishing.com

For distributor details and how to order please visit the 'Ordering' section on our website.

ISBN: 978 1 78535 254 6
Library of Congress Control Number: 2015954381

A CIP catalogue record for this book is available from the British Library.

Design: Stuart Davies

Printed and bound by CPI Group (UK) Ltd, Croydon, CR0 4YY, UK

We operate a distinctive and ethical publishing philosophy in all
areas of our business, from our global network of authors to
production and worldwide distribution.

CONTENTS

What if you slept? And what if, in your sleep, you dreamed? And what if, in your dream, you went to heaven and there plucked a strange and beautiful flower? And what if, when you awoke, you had that flower in your hand? Ah, what then?
– SAMUEL TAYLOR COLERIDGE

To learn how to die is to learn how to live; to learn how to live is to learn how to act not only in this life, but in the lives to come. To transform yourself truly and learn how to be reborn as a transformed being to help others is really to help the world in the most powerful way of all.
– SOGYAL RINPOCHE

The Committee is concerned about the situation of children born of Catholic priests, who, in many cases, are not aware of the identity of their fathers... The Committee recommends that the Holy See assess the number of children born of Catholic priests, find out who they are and take all the necessary measures to ensure the rights of these children to know and to be cared for by their fathers, as appropriate. The Committee also recommends that the Holy See ensure that churches no longer impose confidentiality agreements when providing mothers with financial plans to support their children
– UNITED NATIONS

If a priest comes to me and tells me that he has gotten a woman pregnant... I remind him that the natural law comes before his right as a priest... just as that child has a right to his mother, he has the right to the face of his father.
– JORGE, CARDINAL BERGOGLIO, CURRENTLY POPE FRANCIS, 2013–PRESENT

For my amazing mother

Foreword

Hannah first contacted me in December 2013 and was trying to make sense of an experience she had when she sustained multiple injuries after falling while on holiday in Tenerife. Hannah is not alone; since I began my research into NDEs over twenty years ago I have received thousands of emails from people who are in a similar situation of trying to understand such a transcendent experience that occurred during life threatening circumstances.

From her email, it was apparent that she already had some insight into her experience and realised that it was an NDE but needed some confirmation or validation. She described classic components of the NDE along with some apparent ongoing life changes that have occurred since her fall. There are many misconceptions about NDEs and many people wrongly assume that an NDE is merely a case of perhaps having an out of body experience and then travelling down a dark tunnel towards a bright light. NDEs are far more complex than that and involve many aftereffects both physical and psychological, as well as drastic changes in values and relationships with others.

This book is not just about Hannah's NDE but also about her (non-existent) relationship with her father. The first chapter gives a background to how she never understood her father's rejection of her and how she had always hoped that one day he would show his love for her. Sadly, this was never to happen and Hannah was deeply affected by this and even more so by the secrecy surrounding her existence in his life which had far-reaching implications that reverberated in Hannah's behaviour in the years leading up to her NDE. However, Hannah's NDE initiated a renewed perspective on the situation which has given her the strength to accept his rejection and she is now able to respond with compassion.

Like many NDEs, Hannah's began with a feeling of disbelief about what was happening – surely she wasn't really leaving her body?? Without giving too much away about Hannah's account of her experience, she described it as a wonderful experience; she didn't want to leave that feeling of unconditional love and peace. By the time she had been taken to hospital she started to regain consciousness. Whilst Hannah was lapsing in and out of consciousness the doctor called her name and it grounded her in this reality, and the NDE began to diminish. She then fought against regaining consciousness because she wanted to continue with what she was experiencing in this altered state of consciousness.

When she finally opened her eyes she was confused by the electric lighting as it was very different from the radiant, love-filled light that she was experiencing while unconscious. Interestingly, like many others I have spoken to, Hannah was sedated during the critical phase of hospital admission and was later able to make a clear distinction between the NDE and the experience of being sedated. NDEs are a heightened state of awareness that have often been described to me by others as being "realer than real" or "true reality"; nothing like the dull, sometimes confusional experiences evoked by some drugs administered.

Hannah's account of her time spent in a foreign hospital is insightful and reiterates how important non-verbal communication is. While lying in bed frightened about what was going on, Hannah described how reassuring and helpful it was when the nurse held her hand reinforcing the importance of touch and compassion; there are no language barriers to meeting our basic human needs. The stages of Hannah's recovery highlight how we can take simple things for granted. She describes how wonderful her first meal tasted, how it felt to have her hair washed and how receiving cards from her friends reiterated how loved she is. She became acutely aware of the kindness of others and how she'd not really noticed this before, and how grateful she was to all of the hospital staff in their efforts to save her life.

Issues that arise for many patients who have been critically ill concern subjective experiences of nightmares and difficulty in sleeping, and Hannah too describes these. She knew these were different to the NDE and she desperately wanted to talk about the NDE but was afraid to mention it to the nurses and doctors in case they put it down to her losing her sanity or the experience just being a hallucination. She tried to explain about the NDE to her mother but, as is usually the case in those who have never even heard of these experiences, it was difficult for her to identify with and understand what her daughter was trying so hard to communicate to her.

When she had been discharged home the NDE took second place to the depression she experienced as she came to terms with the feelings of guilt evoked by the events around her fall. The enormity of what had happened hit hard which was helped by the counselling received and eventually the depression lifted.

As part of understanding her NDE, Hannah began reading accounts of other people's NDEs which were a big help. These well-known cases of NDEs were insightful and crucial for her integration process. Many NDE accounts she read conveyed the importance of unconditional love and Hannah realised that she hadn't loved herself up until the point of her NDE. Then began the life changes; her attitude to spirituality changed and her previous beliefs were all instantaneously discarded as a result of what she experienced during her NDE and she began asking all sorts of questions.

Like many others who have had an NDE, Hannah too found that her experience had opened her up to a greater 'psychic awareness' and further in the book she describes an experience that resulted in her returning home earlier than planned and finding her mother seriously unwell and requiring hospitalisation.

The long-term effects of Hannah's NDE have been far reaching and have included a much-improved relationship with her mother. Her life has completely changed and she believes that her NDE has now given her life meaning, direction and purpose. When she was in hospital she knew that she wanted to go to university to study and she has done exactly that. Hannah now works as an art teacher and has trained to be a counsellor. She met her future husband and they married and now have three children; all of whom she is very proud.

An extremely important stage of Hannah's recovery appeared to happen when she met a counsellor who had an understanding of spirituality. Hannah later became aware of a support group for others who were in a similar situation to Hannah with their fathers. She felt a sense of community and realised that she was not alone and not the only person to be rejected by their father. Reading the accounts of others who were in a similar position was very helpful especially as her new insights gained from her NDE were beginning to have a positive influence on the situation.

Coming to terms with an NDE is a process that can take many years and in some cases decades. The life changes can be so drastic that it can impact on relationships with others in ways both positive and negative. There are also healing effects of an NDE and this appears to be happening with the situation with Hannah and her father. The NDE has given Hannah the strength to understand the rejection of her father, and the self-love she developed from her NDE has given her the ability to cope with this. As she has mentioned, this is a work in progress but she is now able to apply compassion to her situation. Thus the NDE has helped foster a loving response towards her father which has been very thera-peutic.

This is a wonderful example of a life transformed after an NDE. Hannah says in the beginning of this book that she now considers the life threatening accident to be the best thing that ever happened to her. I have heard this so many times from other people who feel that their lives too have been changed by their NDE. Hannah wants to communicate this renewed perspective of life and her new understanding that we are all in charge of our own destiny to others – especially her children. She now applies these new insights she has gained and makes positive, conscious life choices.

Not only has writing this book has been cathartic for Hannah, it has also conveyed a very inspiring story of healing and transformation that we can all take heed of. She is in the process of finding meaning and a deeper understanding of the relationship with her father and as a result of her NDE is now making peace with the situation. Her underlying message is that ultimately everything is about love; how wonderful our world would be if everyone realised this.

Dr Penny Sartori, author of *The Wisdom of Near-Death Experiences*

Introduction

In January 1998, I was injured in an accident, sustaining life threatening multiple injuries. During the many months of healing and recovery that followed, I often felt that my life had been cataclysmically shattered and that I would never feel happy or at peace again. But now, seventeen years on, I see the accident as the best thing that ever happened to me. It was a catalyst for a series of changes and life events, amazing and excruciating in equal measure, that stand out as turning points in a life-transforming journey.

There are two facts inextricably bound up with all this that I should mention at the outset. The first is that in 1978 my father chose to become a Catholic priest, omitting to tell anyone arranging his ordination that he'd just separated from my mother and had a one month old baby daughter (me). He embarked on a plan to keep me a secret, which he still tries to uphold to this day. The second fact is that directly after the accident, while still 'unconscious', I had what has become known as a near-death experience. I am very aware of how much scepticism surrounds the reporting of near-death experiences, or NDEs as I'll call them from now on, and in writing my account I am in no way seeking to prove the true nature or validity of them. I am just hoping to share my story as truthfully and accurately as possible. I now see that these two facts, my father's actions and my NDE, are interconnected and I hope to deepen my understanding of how and why this is through the process of writing, while also sharing my experience as I now realise there are people out there who have been through a similar thing and might benefit from knowing they are not alone.

During the darkest times, other people's accounts of how NDEs had transformed their lives often kept me going and gave me hope. I would now like to add to that literature, and if my book helps just one person in a similar way I'll be very happy. The most inspirational NDE account I've read and one that has massively helped me have the courage to speak up has been Anita Moorjani's, in her book *Dying To Be Me: My Journey from Cancer, to Near Death, to True Healing.* Her words helped me find the courage to start writing this book, although in some ways the idea of it being published is terrifying, not least because my mother and I have received veiled threats over the years from my father, warning us not to upset his web of secrecy, or "great losses will result". These threats will be discussed in more detail later on.

I have always found the conflict between the civilised and rational letters from Catholic priests known to me at odds with the actuality of their behaviour. I am hoping that by including many of the letters in this book, the true nature of the situation will come to the fore. Having been handed snippets of information throughout my life, and at times being given letters from people involved years after they were written, so that the emotions they evoke in me do not occur at the time of the described actions, it makes a coherent timeline of events and reactions sometimes hard to envisage. Therefore I feel my perception and the true nature of everything that happened from my conception to now is blurred and has gaps. I am hoping that by using the letters I have been given from my father, senior priests and a cardinal as primary source information, they will act as building blocks for me to piece together the rest of the years as accurately as possible.

I have no wish to hurt anyone through my writing or to produce a sensational exposé so will change all relevant names, not because I'm protecting my father and the Catholic Church but because I want to write the book from a place of love that studies all actions to gain understanding and not revenge. That said, I feel very strongly that I no longer want to be silenced and that it is the right time to explore and be honest about my own life without censor.

Note to reader: My use of the word "God" throughout this book also stands for every other name for God that there is, for the most powerful universal power. I don't mean, through use of the word "God", to confine words solely in the Christian tradition; I mean the term to symbolise the greatest power that there is, inclusively.

Chapter One

Early Years

I met my father for the first time when I was fourteen. It was Autumn, a time of year I've always looked forward to: the darkening evenings and crisp mornings heralding the exciting run-up to Christmas.

Between September 1989 and July 1996 I lived at a boarding school in the countryside during the week, having gained a scholarship there when I was eleven, going home to South East London most weekends. It was the school who organised a counsellor to come with me to meet my father, James Carson, for the first time. It was suggested to me by school staff that I shouldn't broadcast the news of my heritage, but to be circumspect in revealing my father's job to any of my friends, a task I agonised about, wanting to share the information so my friends and I could talk about it but unsure of what might happen if I did. In the end I decided to just confide in my best friend.

During the days before the first meeting, my wider group of friends (who knew I was going to meet my father for the first time but understood him to be a lecturer not a priest) and I eagerly discussed probable outcomes of the meeting. They offered various opinions such as,

"He'll probably cry when he sees you."

"It will be like it is on television, where the two relatives who've never met before run towards each other, crying."

"He'll really love you and wish he'd got to know you sooner."

Buoyed up by the fantasy we'd created and daydreaming about various positive outcomes, I eagerly looked forward to the meeting and was very glad when the day arrived. The counsellor chosen by the school wasn't qualified, but was the husband of a teacher who had an interest in psychology. Looking back, it might have been better if he had been a 'she', as I had trouble trusting men, perhaps due to the absence of my father. Nevertheless, the nuns at the school were very kind to me and did their best, and I know the choice of counsellor was made with kindness. Psychologist Dr Linda Nielsen writes, "The quality of a daughter's relationship with her father is always affecting her relationships with men – either in good ways or in bad ways… When a woman doesn't trust men, can't maintain an ongoing relationship, doesn't know how to communicate, or is co-dependent, this is probably because her relationship with her father lacked trust and/or communication." This was definitely true of me at that point.

I'll come back to the first meeting with my father soon but first I think it's worth looking more deeply at the events which led up to it. At the age of two I had no idea that most people at least knew or knew of their father. I was perfectly happy with my mother and, as children do, just accepted that everything was how it should be. When I was about three I must have become aware that there were such things as fathers, as I remember asking my mum if one of her male friends was my father. My mother never had another serious relationship after my father left her so there was never a man living with us as I grew up.

As I grew older and became more inquisitive, noticing that everyone else I knew spent time with their fathers even if their parents were divorced, I asked more questions and was told my father was a university lecturer who lived in London. The drive to find out who he really was ballooned at this point until I felt I simply must know, as not knowing was too painful. Professor Patricia Casey says of priests' children who don't know the identity of their father, "It seems the big issue is the secret of it. Even if they are misled they might have a sense that something is not quite right."[1] During a weekend home from school at the age of twelve I must have been particularly persistent and curious as it was then that my mum told me he was a Catholic priest. I went back to school feeling very confused, feeling this was not quite right but not knowing why. I was in no doubt that this was a secret I should keep largely to myself.

My mother, Emma, was born in 1943, the fourth of five children, and grew up in a traditional Catholic household in Surrey. Her mother was a headmistress and her father an accountant; I think it would be fair to say that she and her brother and sisters all recall their childhood differently, some have happy memories, others not so much. The Catholic Church played a huge part in her upbringing, and she and her siblings all became involved with it throughout their lives to varying degrees.

My mother met my father in the common room of a London university where they were both studying, she for a theology degree and James in a seminary with the view to becoming a priest. They were in a relationship for around two years, during which time my father told my mother he was considering not becoming a priest. Opinions about whether their relationship was ethical or moral will obviously vary greatly. My father was not a priest at the time although he was in training – two of my mother's flatmates were also in relationships with men destined for the priesthood, but both these men left the seminary, married their girlfriends, had children and remain married to this day. Was my mother wrong for getting together with my father? Was my father wrong for getting into a relationship with my mother? I don't think there are any definitive answers to these questions as different conclusions can be drawn depending on which belief system you judge them by, for example perhaps devout Catholics would feel differently about it than non-Catholics. Anita Moorjani made an interesting point when she said, "anything that is 'true' has to be universal – in that, it has to apply to everyone, and not leave anyone out. Any religion that only applies to some and not others is not 'true'. Truth applies to all."[2]

I think my mother and father's individual motives for getting into the relationship probably come closest to right and wrong choices. Their reactions after it was discovered that my mother was pregnant with me probably point to their different intentions; my mother seemed genuinely in love with my father and was hurt by his reaction, whereas he immediately distanced himself from her, indicating, perhaps, that the situation was alright with him (a last hurrah?) as long as it was problem free.

It was not problem free, however, if my conception and birth are to be considered problematic. When my mother confided to my father that she was pregnant, he was less than overjoyed. Aghast, appalled and horrified would be a more accurate description. He was from a very Catholic family himself, and I have come to understand that he was the favoured child of three. His upbringing was middle class and I think it would be accurate to say that his mother had great aspirations for him. A Catholic mother of Irish heritage would no doubt have been very proud of her only son entering the priesthood, an occupation that Wikipedia categorizes as upper-middle class. James announcing that he'd impregnated a fellow student would no doubt have dented the proceedings somewhat. Did he genuinely believe he was destined to serve God? And if so, why was his behaviour towards my mother so opposite to that of a celibate priest? The answers to these questions can only be guessed at.

In 1977, when my mother was about three months pregnant, James asked her to attend a meeting with himself and his mentor, a senior priest, Father Frank Harding. I have recently been given documents that provide two conflicting accounts of this meeting. Father Frank Harding wrote the following account to a cardinal in June 1996.

Dear Cardinal,
Thank you for your letter. It may be useful for me to write this very brief, incomplete note.
In... 1977 I was asked to help with James' and Emma's consideration of the way ahead, once it was clear Emma was pregnant. Discussions went on over several weeks. Both of them came individ-

ually to see me, and they came together for a joint meeting.

I and many others have never taken the fact of pregnancy in itself a good necessity-making reason for people to get married; and it was evident that marriage between Emma and James wasn't in prospect. So for James there seemed basically two possibilities: getting a job and being a normal separated father; or proceeding to diaconal ordination (fixed for June 1977) and priesthood.

I, when asked, put the view to each of them individually that priesthood could be viable, but only if there was an agreed framework of lives apart, the father's anonymity etc. Emma indicated to me readiness for the latter path. At the joint meeting Emma expressed encouragement to James to continue to the diaconal ordination and to priesthood, assuring him that she would uphold the framework described. Any communication would be through myself. Given all this, James came to regard his proceeding to ordination as right.

God bless,

Father Harding

The suggestion that my mother happily encouraged my father on towards priesthood is refuted in the following letter, written by her to the Cardinal in May 1998.

Dear Cardinal,

Thank you for your letter. My own position will hopefully be clarified through the following points:

In your letter you say I had a relationship with a priest in 1977. James… was not a priest or even a deacon then. He was on a shortened course for mature candidates. His behaviour in his relationship with me was not priestly at any time.

With reference to another of your points, I agree that with hindsight the decisions taken were wrong. At the time I felt them to be wrong. Never at any time did I think James should go forward into the priesthood given the circumstances and his nature.

Please take the following points very seriously:

In 1977, James never discussed with me on my own what we should do. All his discussions seemed to be with Father Harding. I never knew what was said in these.

I knew I was pregnant from March 1977. From April until after his exams in June, I agreed that he could study and we would wait until after that to discuss what should be done. He refused to discuss it with me when the time came.

I was unaware, at that time, of the extent of his friendship with Father Harding. He insisted that I come to "have a short chat" with Father Harding. I did not want to do this. I thought we should be sorting it out ourselves but I went as he was so insistent.

The chat turned out to be a meeting to which James came to fully prepared with several sheets of A4 paper containing his choices, totally undiscussed with me.

I had no idea that this was the meeting where a final and conclusive decision was to be made. In no way was I ready for that. I had been in a state of shock and bewilderment since finding out I was pregnant. I could not understand why James would not discuss the situation with me.

He started the meeting by saying, "Of course marriage is out of the question," (his words). This had never previously been discussed.

The only choice I wanted was that we should wait until after the baby was born until any decision was made. This was rejected immediately without discussion as he said he had a date for his ordination.

James was looking for black and white answers in a situation that had none and in which rushed decisions could not be made.

I was not being listened to, and it suddenly became obvious to me that since April he had been desperately extricating himself out of any responsibility. By this point I was too hurt to listen any more.

He went on reading from his notes. All the choices were his. He had no right then and has no right now to say that any part of the decision was mine. Such a decision only he could make and through his neglectful and cowardly actions through the previous months he had in practice already made it.

How dare he then try to foist on to me the responsibility for making his decision for him about how he was going to respond to his baby? I had already made my decision about my own response.

The outcome of this meeting seems to have decided how my life path went, for a while at least, until I was old enough to assert my own ideas.

Father Frank Harding, now deceased, provoked very different reactions at different times in his life. He has been described as charismatic and electrifying and at one time was hugely popular; however, was accused of sexually abusing young men in 1995. I have no idea whether he was actually guilty or not as there wasn't enough evidence to prove the abuse, but what has become obvious, after reading the letters he sent to my mother, is that he definitely possessed a gift for spinning webs of secrecy.

Following the 1977 meeting, my mother felt coerced and bullied. I think she struggled with the concept of standing up for herself against such a powerful institution. She has told me that during the meeting, Father Harding suggested she went to stay by the sea until the baby arrived, then give it up for adoption. She said no, luckily for me. After the meeting, she wasn't allowed to meet my father properly again – bar one meeting when I was three – for over thirteen years and any communication between the two of them had to go through Father Harding, as stated in his letter. My mother moved in with two friends in North London, who later became my godparents and who we lived with when I was very young. She then had the task of trying to come to terms with the betrayal of a man she loved.

When I was two we moved to a Housing Association flat in South East London. We lived there until I was eight and I remember this as being a very happy time; we were in a large block of flats and I made friends with several of the children who also lived there. It was fun running from my flat to theirs and then playing together in the estate's playground. My memories in that flat form a beautiful patchwork of birthdays, Christmas times, hugs, hamsters, cousins, visits to grandparents, a black and white television, our balcony filled with flowers, a hippy-style rug and a mainly peaceful atmosphere. Occasionally an air of sadness would permeate our flat; I don't know whether it was just me who felt it, or whether my mother felt down at times and I picked up on it. We hardly had any money, my father had not initially sent any until it was pointed out that legal advice would be sought, and worrying about whether money will stretch to the end of the month is exhausting. However, my childhood was very happy and infused with love at all times, from my mother but also from my grand-parents, aunts, uncles and cousins on her side.

I must have started to question my father's whereabouts a bit around the age of seven, because a good friend of my mother's, a priest, wrote the following letter to Father Harding on her behalf.

Dear Frank,

I had a good long talk with Emma last Saturday, which we both found very clarifying and helpful. In our previous rather brief opportunity for a chat, either she had not made herself very clear or I had misunder-stood her. So I would like to set out the position again, afresh.

Now that Hannah has started to ask questions, Emma has to foresee what may happen in the future and prepare her own mind and that of others involved. It may not prove necessary to tell Hannah, but Emma thinks it very likely that it will, a child demands at least a name, and can be given a made-up one; a young adult will demand a particular, real person to relate to mentally – whether to accept, or reject, or any other attitude.

Emma knows she gave an undertaking not to make public who Hannah's father is but, understandably, she feels she gave the under-taking under very considerable pressure, and judges that, while doing her best to bring no harm to anyone else, she must put Hannah's needs first – real needs of identity and self-acceptance, not just curiosity.

She does not consider that to give Hannah the information in some ten years' time, should that prove necessary, would be to make the matter public. There is no reason to suppose Hannah will be less trust-worthy than she (Emma) is supposed to be.

In view of this Emma would like to know two things:

Whether, should the need arise in two or three years' time, J would be willing to see her (Emma) and discuss the matter.

Whether at a later date, and should the need arise, he would be willing to see Hannah, so that the latter would have a definite person in her mind and not some fantasy person.

All good wishes...

I think many facts can be gleaned from this letter. It's clear how impossible it was for my mother to communicate with my father about simple concepts such as can our daughter be told your real name. It is also clear that although she agreed to maintain the web of secrecy to the degree that she was considering not telling me my father's name, she'd felt under pressure to agree to the plan in the first place. Having to ask permission at all shows what a hold my father and the Church had over her, and how fearful she must have been to carry on the secrecy against her better judgement. It's impressive to see that even in the difficult position she was in, my mum continued to fight to establish some sort of connection between myself and my father, an extremely courageous thing to do under the circumstances.

When I was eight my mother bought a tiny two-bedroom flat in a converted Victorian mansion in a better part of town. This was also a happy time, but as is normal with growing daughters and their mothers, friction started to rear its head too. Holidays by the sea at my grandparents' house in Sussex were always a high point and I have many happy memories of playing on the shingly beach with my cousins. It's worth pointing out that no matter how many arguments my mum and I've had, I've always known she's the most amazing mother in the world: strong, courageous, patient and very kind, and I hope she knows that about herself too.

After being told more about my father's identity at the age of twelve I remember expressing a desire to meet him. With the single-minded determination of a hot-headed child who has a bee in her bonnet I pursued this desire until my mother took action. At that age I saw things in black and white; I had a father, I didn't know him for reasons I couldn't really fathom, he was still alive and well, therefore we should meet up so he could get to know me and realise how great I was. Simple. His occupation as a priest didn't overly impress me or seem like a big deal; I've been born with rebellion in every bone in my body and had begun to question the validity of organised religion well before I knew he was a priest. It seemed like a job, like any other job such as being a doctor, teacher or plumber. I had no idea that priests view themselves as living in a "hermetical world set apart and set above the non-ordained members of the Catholic Church."[3] In no way did I expect the fact that he was a priest to stand in the way of our future relationship. We were both human, first and foremost, so why worry about an occupation.

Judging from the letters that document the attempts made at arranging my first meeting with my father, it was no simple or easy task. In fact just arranging one meeting took years.

My mother wrote to Father Harding in 1990 asking whether James would be willing to meet me.

His reply, dated October 1990, reads,

Dear Emma,
Thank you for your letter which has been carefully considered. The situation for Hannah is not easy, nor is it for you. On the under-standing to which James adheres, it is in the circumstances impossible and inappropriate for there to be anything like an involved, normal father-daughter relationship. So it's not in Hannah's best interests...
that anything be done liable to foster in her feelings, desires or thoughts which cannot be met. And a meeting in the coming period would be so liable.

James sees as a more constructive move – much freer of hazards and ramifications – to help Hannah towards more balanced and peaceful perceptions, the arrangement of opportunity for quiet, informal talk between Hannah and me. (After you spoke more to Hannah about her father, some strands of negativity re me may have occurred within her; but any such strands, even if around at all, must be much milder and less tricky than her position vis-à-vis her father.)

James would certainly be ready much later on (maybe even as near as about five years' time) to go into the question of a meeting with Hannah.

God bless,

Frank

I find it interesting to consider how politely Father Frank Harding rebuffs my mother's suggestion that her daughter meet her father. It is hard to think of another profession where it would be deemed permissible to split up natural ties in this way, and for a father's refusal to meet his daughter to be condoned and encouraged. It begs the question, was this an OK thing to do? Not just in the eyes of the Catholic Church but in any eyes? Disregarding any religious dogma and thinking about a bigger picture, is it actually ethical to encourage separation between a father and daughter on religious grounds? I suppose the answer depends entirely on your own views. Personally, I've never been able to reconcile the rejection of a child in the name of the Church as acceptable.

I wasn't aware that my father had refused to see me in 1990, which was probably for the best, although I remember flatly refusing to meet Father Harding on my own when the suggestion was put to me. I never liked him, for reasons I can't fully explain. His eyes were unkind and I did not get a good feeling around him. We met up with him once a year until I was old enough to object, and I remember him taking us to the theatre when I was about five and staring at me without smiling in a way that made me uncomfortable.

To her credit, my mother did not give up her attempts to open communication between myself and my father, and wrote another letter to Father Harding about it in 1991. By then she'd decided it might be a constructive move for them to talk about the situation in the presence of a credible counsellor and put this to Father Harding, perhaps hoping that by including an unbiased third party her voice might be heard more. I, meanwhile, was blissfully unaware that all this communication was flying back and forth. Unfortunately I'm only in possession of one of my mother's letters.

Father Harding sent one backdated October 1991 which reads,

Dear Emma,

This is taking further the question of you and James talking together with a counsellor. James regrets the wait, due to various factors, including recently my absence in the USA.

James sees you and he being able to talk together in a comfortable and constructive way as very desirable. A suitable counsellor could prove useful… Every care to foster anonymity would be important. The agreement would be an agreed revision of, not of course an end of, the existing pattern.

A person who, so it seems to James, would have particularly valuable experience and qualities is Dr Michael Jamison… Obviously, in the circumstances, going into a business of meetings with a counsellor James doesn't know requires my assistance. I've contacted Michael Jamison, indicated (without names etc) the special need for anonymity, and asked if he could meet with the two persons. He says yes. He says I should inquire of both of you about timing.

God bless you,

Frank

Several points come to mind when I read this letter. Firstly, it looks more encouraging in that within less than the five years suggested in the previous letter from Father Harding, my father is willing to discuss meeting me. So that sounds promising, although having to persuade a father to meet up with his own daughter has always struck me as bizarre. Secondly, the need for secrecy and anonymity is blatantly stressed. The priests involved evidently believed it was their right to act in this way, so was it alright? I think if one is immersed in clerical life in the Catholic Church to the point where it becomes your universe and your truth, then covering up priestly transgressions that go against expected life choices such as chastity is probably seen as more favourable and tasteful than openly admitting what you've done. But this throws up a problem for me. Because surely if you were as genuinely good and true as you want people to believe you are then you wouldn't have transgressed in the first place. Or you would have integrity and wouldn't see your actions as a problem, standing by them, and therefore would not need to cover them up. For me, covering up the existence of your child and not being honest with your colleagues and congregation about who you really are are actions that smack of hypocrisy. Throughout my life, this point has been one that has been the most hard to come to terms with and reconcile. How can a man be respected who acts in a devious way? How can you represent the Catholic Church as a priest and preach about love, family and loving your neighbour as you love yourself when your actions in your personal life show anything but that? Is image really more important than integrity? Does it matter more to 'appear' honest than to actually be honest? And what is all this teaching the child who is the result of this hidden union? I don't know the answers to these questions but what has become clear through the Church's actions is that to them the child's psychological well-being is not as important as keeping him or her a secret. Perhaps as a result of all the secrecy I can't stand deviousness in my own life to this day and prefer to be as blunt and open as possible, probably to extremes at times.

Father Harding's letter also indicates that they have conceded to my mother's suggestion that she and James meet with a counsellor. James' choice of counsellor, Dr Michael Jamison, was a well-known psychiatrist and theologian.

My mother must have replied to Father Harding's letter quickly, because he wrote again in October 1991.

> *Dear Emma,*
>
> *Thank you for your letter. Regarding dates. Michael Jamison does not do Saturdays and is very full up till after Christmas. He offers a choice of two dates in January 1992... Either is alright for James, so that if you can fit in, that has not been too difficult to arrange. Can you let me know as soon as you can so that I can finalise with the secretary?*
>
> *As regards the points you raised: a) I gather James' letter to you said you would be hearing more, he didn't comment on who would write. b) I'm sure you should not worry about expense at this stage – it may even be on the NHS. c) The phrase in my letter about "existing pattern" simply reflects James' point that an agreement that you and he meet with Michael Jamison stands in its own right, free as such from implications. d) While indeed many counsellors would have emptier diaries than Michael Jamison, James – prompted by your own letter back in August saying to him "the counsellor could be your choice" – reckons it important to get the right person. Though a bit slow, fixing the appointment has been quite straightforward.*
>
> *My love and prayers,*
> *God bless you,*
> *Frank*

My mother was clearly in contact with my father through letters by this stage, although Father Harding still acted as the 'gatekeeper' for all decisions, blocking any unwanted ones from my mother and protecting my father. His ambiguous remark about the meeting being "free as such from implications" which is offered to explain his previous remark, "The agreement would be an agreed revision of, not of course an end of, the existing pattern" implies that although James has agreed to meet with my mother, he and Father Harding have already decided that the "existing pattern", i.e. the way he goes about his life and the way he acts towards me, will not change or be up for discussion.

Another letter is sent from Father Harding soon after this one, dated November 1991:

Dear Emma,

How time goes… Now, as regards Michael Jamison. I asked him if he would be ready to facilitate the man and woman in question coming to be able to talk about pertinent matters in a constructive manner. He is aware that there is a thirteen year old daughter who is at the heart of the whole situation, and that there is a request that the man meet the daughter. I didn't go into anybody's detailed aims. I am sure that in so far as aims need further attention, that should now be left until you and James can actually talk about it together with Michael Jamison.

God bless you,

Frank

The language has become more secretive, rather cloak and dagger: "the man and woman in question", "there is a request that the man meet the daughter". I wonder why he couldn't just use our names? Again it leads me back to the question, if James hadn't done anything wrong then why the big cover-up? Or does that point to the fact that something unsavoury had actually occurred?

In the nicest possible way, Father Harding goes on to give my mother an instruction: "I am sure that in so far as aims need further attention, that should now be left until you and James can actually talk about it together with Michael Jamison." Don't contact James or I again with your thoughts, leave them for the meeting.

Father Harding sent another letter in January 1992.

Dear Emma,

Now – Dr Jamison's secretary has sent me this map which arrived this

a.m. I hope you will find it helpful on Monday... As I have made all
the arrangements without mentioning any names other than my own
(anonymity in such matters is an aim) – the appointment might be
booked under my name...

Anyhow, I hope this eases your finding the way.
God bless,
Frank

So my mother and father met up together after fifteen years, and
the meeting was presided over by Michael Jamison.
Unfortunately there is then a gap in the correspondence I
possess, with the next letter dated February 1996.

The meeting must have been deemed a success, because the
counsellor chosen by my school, David, and I caught the train to
London in the autumn of 1992 and made our way to London and
found Dr Michael Jamison's office.

We were met warmly by Dr Jamison, who showed us into his
study, which was on the first or second floor of an old building.
There was an air of excitement and expectation in the room. My
father had not yet arrived.

I could hardly speak due to nerves. Being in a room with two
men I hardly knew caused a slice of fear to appear next to the antic-
ipation and excitement already filling me to the brim. The situation
seemed surreal, the office felt like a very masculine environment
full of dark colours and important-looking books. My head swam
and all the questions I'd been planning to ask had evaporated. We
waited for about ten minutes, then the door opened and my father
walked in.

He didn't look like a priest to me, although what does a priest
look like? Maybe what I mean is that I was expecting him to wear
robes he would have worn in church, but he just wore normal,
smart casual clothes. I was wearing turquoise and white tie-dye
jeans from Camden Market, which I thought were absolutely the
best piece of clothing ever invented. From the start James was very

self-possessed and gave away no emotion. He had short grey hair and I remember his eyes being trained on to me from the moment he walked into the room.

I was fully aware that I was now in a room with three men I didn't know, and because of this panic rose up inside me but I didn't let it show. I've always found trusting men very hard. I just sat there, hardly able to speak. My father came and sat very close to me and said,

"Hello, Hannah." He was smiling. I have to be honest and say that I didn't have a good feeling being near him; it made me uncomfortable. There was no warmth; there was a calm civility.

"Hello," I said. For some reason it was at that moment that I realised none of the fantasy my friends and I had constructed was going to come true. As a result, I no longer wanted to be there.

James talked in a slow way, asking questions and telling me little facts about himself. I honestly can't remember exactly what he said, I was so dizzy. Every now and again my counsellor and Dr Jamison would speak, but I can't remember anything they said either.

At some point, James said, "Do you have any questions you want to ask me, Hannah?"

I asked the one burning question that was on my mind.

"Do I have any brothers or sisters?"

He looked me right in the eyes and smiled.

"No," he said smiling, shaking his head. "Absolutely not, I can promise you that." He was so sincere and controlled. I thought it was a real shame that there were no brothers and sisters I could get to know. Even to this day I would be overjoyed to discover I have a half sibling somewhere in the world.

He started talking again, and the gist of what he was saying seemed to be about some things in life just not being possible. James uses complex, verbose language and never chooses the simplest way of explaining anything, a fact since agreed by others who know him. After a while, he said something like,

"So I don't think we should meet again for a few years. Perhaps we could arrange something when you're older. Is that alright with you, Hannah?"

"Yep," I said, because I didn't know what was going on, I just badly wanted to get out of there. An avalanche of thoughts was crashing downwards in my head until only a numb plateau remained. The 2011 Child First document states that "premature imposition of responsibility on the child"[4] and "unrealistic or inappropriate expectations of the child's capacity to understand something" are both indicators of emotional abuse. I don't know whether there's a correlation between these points and my inability to comprehend why my father, because of his position as a priest, could not get to know me and love me unconditionally, but I say with certainty that I still don't understand to this day why "clericalism" as "a situation where priests live in a hermetical world set apart and set above the non-ordained members of the Catholic Church"[5] is an ethical reason to reject your own child. It could be argued that James wasn't rejecting me, and that he had taken "all the necessary measures to ensure the rights of [his child] to know and to be cared for by [her father], as appropriate" as advised by the United Nations, in that he met me once and continued to send my mother regular payments. But these payments, as my father disclosed in a letter dated 24th August 1998, were on the understanding that my mother and I continued to keep quiet about his identity.

From time to time… I've remarked on an obvious, inexorable point: I can produce these sums of money only so long as I still have an income – enabling that; so were an adverse change in my life's circumstances to be impelled, then it'd be liable not to be possible for the above statements about future sums to hold. With the best will in the world, that obvious inexorable point continues.

Basically, if you blab the money dries up, a point made again on the

1st December 1998:

> *An obvious, significant point (which over the years I've voiced to you)*
> *stands… I can produce sums of money only so long as I have an*
> *income – enabling that. If anything were to cause an adverse change*
> *in the circumstances of my life, then it'd be liable not to be possible for*
> *me to send money spoken of. Other aspects of my life and money are*
> *inexorably interlocked. With the best will in the world, that obvious*
> *point holds.*

It is interesting to note that the UN stated: "The Committee also recommends that the Holy See ensure that churches no longer impose confidentiality agreements when providing mothers with financial plans to support their children." Although my mother never signed a confidentiality agreement, the money was certainly sent on the understanding that she and I helped my father remain anonymous.

On the train back to school my counsellor kept asking me how I felt. I was unsure whether I ever wanted to speak again, so ignored him. I felt awful, but I didn't know why. My father had smiled a lot and been very civilised. But confusingly at no point did I feel any warmth or love from him, and talking to him was like playing psychological chess. I'd constantly felt outmanoeuvred. Later I wondered whether he *had* felt anything, any twinge or regret, or wish to see me more often, or perhaps had shown some emotion I didn't pick up on. When all things are considered, though, it seems unlikely.

"I'm fine," I said eventually. I wished David would shut up and leave me alone so I could sort out my fragmented thoughts in peace, but he wanted a response.

"Do you feel rejected?" he asked, quite forcefully. Although at the time it annoyed me that he asked this, it now interests me, because that's obviously what he thought my father had done: rejected me. Now I'm glad he asked that, because it gives me a concrete piece of evidence to remember that backs up how I felt in the months after the meeting, and shows that by using smiles and clever language my father had managed to convey he did not want to continue to get to know me in person. But on the train on the way home I just said, "No," because having a tiny bit of control over how I answered questions felt like a small victory in a less than victorious day. It probably came across as rude but I was past caring.

I know that my father would give a very different account of the meeting; perhaps to him it went well. He played his part, he met me, was very polite and provided a little information about his life, then in a civilised way explained that it would be best all round if we didn't meet again for a few years. Where's the harm in that?

Unfortunately the harm started to manifest itself very soon.

How do you tell your friends your father doesn't want to see you again for several years? Suspecting that if you do this implies that there's something inherently wrong with you? I think I told them that everything was fine, and at that age, children don't probe too deeply. I do remember that I was consumed with a terrible feeling that I was worthless from that moment onwards and my diary entries became very angry and depressed. If your father has never met you and rejects you, that's less painful because secretly you know he would love you if he ever met you. But when he meets you and still doesn't love you, that's when it hurts. I threw all my diaries away a few years ago as I felt the angst in them was something I didn't want to hoard all my life, although I've always written things down in one form or another, as writing's very cathartic.

I don't think I enjoyed the run-up to Christmas all that much that year and an anger was growing inside me that I didn't understand and had no control over. It was an odd situation. I told everyone I was fine but my thoughts about it all were either numb or disjointed. Dr Jamison had thought my father a jolly fine fellow and it was confusing to feel the opposite of what adults are telling you. Unfortunately, perhaps as a result of me being away at school most of the time, my mother and I were no longer so close. I think that to be happy at boarding school you have to detach yourself somewhat from loved ones at home to some degree, because if you didn't you'd be constantly homesick. For the next few years we continued to grow apart.

Life went on as normal, although I couldn't sleep. I would lie awake night after night with my thoughts racing, not thinking about anything in particular, but it was like my brain had been put on an electronic hamster wheel and ramped up to top speed. Eventually I went to the school doctor and explained I was having real trouble sleeping and he told me to put lavender in my pillow and sniff it at night and it would relax me. I put lavender in my pillow and sniffed it but it didn't make the blindest bit of difference. In hindsight I think I was becoming depressed. Psychiatrist Professor Patricia Casey, who is based at UCD and the Mater Misericordiae Hospital, says: "that somebody who was conceived by a priest would feel a strong sense of estrangement and emptiness,"[6] and that was certainly true of me at this time.

I still enjoyed being with my friends, I joined in with after school clubs such as gymnastics and dance and I looked forward to my favourite subjects such as art and English literature (I wanted to be a writer when I was grown up). I knew I had a fantastic mum who, although she was tired and only saw me most weekends, was trying her very best. But all the time there was something at the back of my mind telling me I was worthless.

In the end I went to see a doctor back home, and asked her for sleeping tablets. She was very reluctant to give them, but in the end gave me two, so I had two very good nights' sleep, then the old pattern reasserted itself. I kept bursting into tears at inappropriate times at school, then excusing myself and going somewhere to hide until I'd calmed down. I remember this happening during a piano lesson and my teacher just looked at me aghast and said, "Darling, no one should be this upset at your age." By 1993 I was studying for my GCSEs. I found it hard to concentrate on revising but ended up getting a mixture of As and Bs.

Going into the sixth form in the autumn term of 1994 was a breath of fresh air, I felt I was moving on. We were housed in a different building, had more privileges and led a freer life. My circle of friends, who I'm still close to now, became everything to me. They were and still are utterly amazing. Being with them, trying new things and questioning rules became a priority. We were certainly getting into the swing of 'being teenagers' and our behaviour was changing accordingly. A *National Geographic* article says:

The first full series of scans of the developing adolescent brain – a National Institutes of Health (NIH) project that studied over a hundred young people as they grew up during the 1990s – showed that our brains undergo a massive reorganization between our 12th and 25th years... Imaging work done since the 1990s shows that these physical changes move in a slow wave from the brain's rear to its front, from areas close to the brain stem that look after older and more behaviourally basic functions, such as vision, movement, and fundamental processing, to the evolutionarily newer and more complicated thinking areas up front... at times, and especially at first, the brain does this work clumsily. It's hard to get all those new cogs to mesh... These studies help explain why teens behave with such vexing inconsistency: beguiling at breakfast, disgusting at dinner; masterful on Monday, sleepwalking on Saturday. Along with lacking experience generally, they're still learning to use their brain's new networks. Stress, fatigue, or challenges can cause a misfire... We're so used to seeing adolescence as a problem. But the more we learn about what really makes this period unique, the more adolescence starts to seem like a highly functional, even adaptive period. It's exactly what you'd need to do the things you have to do then.[7]

There we go, our new behaviour and the questioning of rules was normal!

By the age of seventeen, my rebellion had started in earnest. My friends and I sometimes sneaked out of school and got the train down to London for a night of hard clubbing, before coming back rather tired the next day. After somehow gaining three modest A-levels with hardly any work, two of my friends and I got into London art colleges and rented a house in South London together. This is when things went a little crazy. Life became a fusion of dry ice, late nights, banging techno, deep house, Cyber Dog clothes, quickly-made new friends, warmth, love, excitement, raves, festivals, Ibiza and neon face paint. We Reclaimed the Streets in Trafalgar Square, we travelled to different parties round London, we went to bed late and got up late. I felt I belonged to a tribe, I could see no end to our fun.

I started an on/off three year tempestuous relationship with a man who periodically broke up with me. After a great start, probably due to our opposing needs and attitudes, it was clear it was never going to work.

For a year or so, my friends and I had an absolute hedonistic blast. "My fondest memory of the 1990s is rave culture. It was punk for my generation who were too young to appreciate previous youth sub cultures. In the early years I'd go to raves in England and meet people from all over the place. I'd travel miles just to go and dance for hours, no one cared what you wore or where you were from because you were there. Anyone could make a record (and they did!) or be a promoter. Sadly Britain rapidly became more apathetic towards the new millennium, (thanks to the Tories Criminal Justice Act amongst other things) and pop culture became a regurgitation of what went on before. Ideal for the oncoming 'Blairism'."[8]

The first letter I have from my father to my mother was from this period, dated February 1996. Some of it has been cut away for mysterious reasons I'm not privy to, but here is an extract from the remaining writing.

> *For you to force me on to the latter path* [which was probably being more open about being my father or perhaps leaving the priesthood], *the results would not be those intended; and it's obscure how the upshot would help Hannah, you, the Diocese, me, people who find me of assistance, or anybody. In saying that I am not – repeat with stress, not – suggesting that such forcing is at all in view. I fully appreciate reticence shown. It just seems wise gently to guard against the slightest possibility of a situation arising where an individual* [meaning my mother or me] *wrings his hands and says, "If only I'd realised before, such-and-such would not have been done." If you, and of course Hannah – and indeed myself – can be relatively free of problems in the period ahead and able to carry on with life peacefully, that seemingly would be valuable all round.*

It seems to me that what James wants here is for Emma to leave him alone and stop asking him to change in his relationship and attitude with me. A gentle threat is included, "if only I'd realised before, such-and-such would not have been done". He wants to be left alone and "relatively free of problems in the period ahead". But it seems to me that by choosing to enter the priesthood without being honest in 1977 and therefore concocting the secrecy plan, at that point my father was helping to create the problems he was asking Emma to stop bothering him with in 1996.

My mother must have written to him again over the next year, perhaps expressing how hurt she'd been at his actions during the meeting of 1977.

He wrote back in May 1996:

Dear Emma,
I want to take very seriously what you're evincing. So much has been extremely difficult for you. Where I'm in no doubt that such-and-such was said or done in 1977, it'd be wrong for me to state blandly now,

"such-and-such was not after all so". You wouldn't welcome my behaving thus. But of course complex things are involved. Beyond what one regards as having been actually said or done in 1977 – or not – points can arise respecting what one sees oneself as having really wanted in 1977, etc, etc. Post 1977 may enter, also... My putting a lot further into writing wouldn't fit. However, given an aim and all round value that as much insight and harmony occur as is achievable, then your and my going into things with Dr Jamison appears worthwhile. Plainly each of us over time has had plenty of negative images and feelings, regrets and pressures: any gratuitous addition of these/sense of being dragooned into a meeting would well be avoided.

With good wishes,

James

Perhaps my mother had voiced her frustration and anger about her treatment in 1977, about being coerced into agreeing to him continuing to the priesthood and the secrecy plan without her one stipulation that they wait until after the baby be born to make a decision being listened to. Perhaps she wanted some parental support, as she was the only one dealing with their wayward child. Perhaps he was still the closest person she had to a partner, the only one to talk about child rearing with, even though they were so estranged. But they seem to have agreed to meet with Dr Michael Jamison. This must have been a productive meeting because nearly a year later, in March 1997, my father wrote to my mother saying,

Of course at Hannah's wish there hasn't to date been the renewed interaction between Hannah and me which you and I spoke of in September. However, our reviewing together of how matters are going might be wise, and I'm definitely ready for a meeting.

Rightly or wrongly, I do find it irritating how the meetings with my father were so minutely discussed behind my back. This possibly contributed to my disinclination to meet him. To this day, I can't stand being controlled or finding myself part of contrived situations. However, it was around this time that I met up with my father again, this time in Kew Gardens, London – his suggestion – which I found out later is where he took my mother when they were together.

We ended up in the garden of a pub, with him buying me copious amounts of alcohol and me getting drunk and maudlin. We met again two or three times over the next year, and I continued to feel like we were playing psychological chess. I also felt like I was being silenced in other ways.

"Do you have any brothers or sisters?"

"Yes, two sisters."

"Can I meet them?" I thought they might want to get to know me.

"No, that wouldn't be appropriate."

"Do they know about me?"

"No."

"Why don't you tell them? They might like to meet me?"

"No, they are both psychologically unstable, I fear news like this would cause their states to worsen, and neither you nor I would want that on our conscience, would we?"

James always used his sisters' alleged 'mental illnesses' as reasons never to tell them about me. Much later on, I did find out that one of his sisters became mentally ill later in life and has now died, the other is still alive and knows nothing of me. But would finding out she had a niece who wanted to get to know her before she died have caused my aunt's condition to worsen, or was it a convenient excuse to continue the secrecy?

I started to devise ways to make him love me. I put together a photo album of pictures of me from birth to the present. I bought books that dealt with people living religious lives having revelations about love and sent them to him. I got drunk on the rare occasions we met and spouted depressing statements in a bid to try and touch a nerve within him. He sat and took it all, smiling and civilised. It became clear that nothing was going to nudge him into having genuine paternal feelings of love and protection, the kind where you would move heaven and earth in order to look after your child. We would always meet in a carefully orchestrated way, that lacked love or any genuine intent. Now that I'm a mother myself, I do struggle to understand how someone could have such a reaction to their own child. I turned this loss on myself, the worthless feeling that had stayed like a tumour since first meeting him in 1992 magnified and ballooned, probably jogged along by my hedonistic lifestyle; usual weekends including lots of dancing and not much food.

My mum recalls that James was emphasising secrecy to me a lot at this point. A letter to her dated August 1996 goes some way to explaining his point of view:

> Apropos of a matter touched on briefly at the end, conceivably it'd be worth my saying again summarily what we went into more in 1992–93. It just is the case that were Hannah to be talking about her father's identity then – given how the imperfect world tends to operate and so on – certain outcomes would be prone to follow; outcomes which Hannah herself now or later in life, as well as other people, might regret. It's extremely unfortunate that that's the case: but the reality is thus... I, of course, will be inviting contact with Hannah, in the way we said.
> Yours sincerely,
> James

In writing this book I am of course hoping the regrettable "certain outcomes" James mentions *don't* happen; I can't think what they would be, I don't like to imagine. One of my aims in writing this book is the hope that it highlights the secrecy many children of priests are forced to live with, and although I feel a tad cautious because of all the civilised, polite intimidations James has included in his letters over the years about unfortunate events happening if

I ever talked, this subject does need to be discussed. I wonder why my father talked about "the imperfect world"? Is his perception of a flawed world the only thing standing in the way of the truth being told?

As psychiatrist Professor Patricia Casey says, "due to the rarity of the situation, no psychiatrist could claim to have expertise in the area"[9] of counselling children of priests, but she says the major issue these children face is secrecy. As these cases are only just starting to be talked about, there is no research I could find into the effect of secrecy on priests' children, but there is much written about the effect of secrecy on children generally.

> Keeping traumatic secrets can result in excessive stress and guilt for the person carrying the burden of knowledge, even when that silence is thought to be the best possible option for all concerned. Physical symptoms such as anxiety, headaches, backaches, and digestive problems often can occur when disturbing secrets are internalized, rather than shared, especially over a long period of time. Persons harboring such discomfort often turn to alcohol, or other addictive substances, to mask their pain. It is important to remember that both the person keeping the secret, as well as those who live with the secret-keeper, including young children, can experience similar physical and mental health issues.[10]

The worse I felt, the worse life got. I didn't eat, my weight dropped, my smallest leggings were baggy. I noticed that whereas my friends were continuing to bounce back after our nights out, still able to go to college and work, I just felt awful the whole time. My college attendance dropped, I was hardly on speaking terms with my mother, I was alienating friends, and trying to combat these awful states of consciousness by pursuing a 'good time' with more and more ferocity. Perhaps there is no correlation between my father's treatment of me and my decline at this time. Maybe there was just something wrong with me. But a psychologist told my mother that "it is a common misunderstanding about abandonment that the abandoned child suffers more than the abandoned adult... the fact is that when the abandoned child becomes an adult the suffering is more intense and painful as the full realisation of what has happened to them dawns." Confusingly, my father hadn't entirely 'abandoned me', because I'd met him about four times by then. I find this statement very interesting:

Living with repeated abandonment experiences creates toxic shame. Shame arises from the painful message implied in abandonment: "You are not important. You are not of value." This is the pain from which people need to heal... Emotional abandonment occurs when parents do not provide the emotional conditions and the emotional environment necessary for healthy development. I like to define emotional abandonment as "occurring when a child has to hide a part of who he or she is in order to be accepted, or to not be rejected." Having to hide a part of yourself means... it is not okay to have needs. Everyone else's needs appear to be more important than yours... Other acts of abandonment occur when... Children are held responsible for other people's behaviour. They may be consistently blamed for the actions and feelings of their parents... Many times abandonment issues are fused with distorted, confused, or undefined boundaries such as... When parents are not willing to take responsibility for their feelings, thoughts, and behaviours, but expect children to take responsibility for them... Abandonment plus distorted boundaries, at a time when children are developing their sense of worth, is the foundation for the belief in their own inadequacy and the central cause of their shame... Abandonment experiences and boundary violations are in no way indictments of a child's innate goodness and value. Instead, they reveal the flawed thinking, false beliefs, and impaired behaviours of those who hurt them.[11]

These words describe how I felt much of the time between the ages of fourteen and twenty. Does being a Catholic priest exonerate you from being guilty of different types of mistreatment? Again, the answer to this probably depends on individual views.

Whatever the reason, my fun period was clearly over. I had stopped looking after myself, and was probably very depressed: drinking too much, not sleeping, partying without any sense of having a good time. Happiness had disappeared with a leaden feeling taking its place. I'd lost my identity; I remember realising one day that I had no sense of individuality, no sense of 'me', there was just an empty void inside me and that was terrifying; dehumanizing. I had no aspirations, I didn't want to be anything career wise. I could remember having an identity when I was younger, and this was painful as I wanted to get it back. I missed my school very much, leaving it was like a bereavement. By the end of 1997 I was in a one-way spiral towards rock bottom, made acutely worse every time my boyfriend dumped me. I just didn't have the skills to get out of the cycle, I was too far in.

In January 1998, my friend Abigail and I flew out to Tenerife for a week of winter sun, paid for with student loans. We'd had a particularly heavy few days of clubbing beforehand and I was at my thinnest, hardly eating anything, not sleeping, drinking too much. I felt anxious, frustrated, stuck, disordered and scared. I wanted to recreate the fun days I'd had in Ibiza with different friends; I think I was trying to find a way to feel good again, but the downward spiral continued relentlessly. It was clearly the choices I was making that were fuelling this spiral and they were made within the context I was in. During the four-hour plane ride I felt trapped and hollow, like a robot having an identity crisis. A very real sense of doom had descended. I wanted to stop my thoughts and get off the plane, but my mind and the journey were relentless.

We stayed in an apartment just up the mountain from Playa de las Américas. "Young people head to Playa de las Américas for its hedonistic appeal; in particular the one kilometre stretch known as Verónicas that is packed with nightclubs, cabaret bars, live music venues, shops and restaurants. Neon lights, music pumping from the doorways and people dancing in the street are what you will find here. It really does come alive at night, every night!"[12] Indeed, although to me it felt like a living hell as soon as we arrived, probably due to my state of mind. Everything felt tacky, wrong and tainted. I'd only known Abigail for three months and felt less connected to her each day.

We went out every night and attempted to have a good time. Lots of alcohol and not much food isn't a winning combination at the best of times. On Friday night we headed out again visiting several bars and clubs along the strip called Veronicas. It was in the last one that I met Rob.

"You look like fun," he said, introducing himself. I didn't feel like fun but any attention was good attention. I smiled, wanting to appear normal.

"What are you drinking?"

"Vodka." Why did I say vodka? I hate vodka.

Rob went to the bar and the barman poured vodka into two enormous glasses, filling them up as though it was water, adding a tiny splash of lemonade afterwards.

I caught sight of myself in a nearby mirror. My eyes looked hollow.

"Here you go," Rob said. I seemed like a good person and I managed a fake grin, which masked rising panic. There were too many people in the club, the club was too small, the music too loud, the lights too confusing. I headed for the door; it was a basement club, so I climbed the stone steps, then fell all the way back down.

"She's a few eggs short of a batch," someone chuckled, as I began the ascent again. The words seemed like a code I couldn't crack. For some reason this bothered me to the core.

This time I achieved the top step successfully, Rob close behind. We sat on a wall in the dark by the sea. It was very cold.

Rob talked but I couldn't talk back. He seemed bemused but he kept smiling and trying to get me to talk. I nodded and tried to grin.

At some point he went and got us another drink each. I drank it and as I finished a veil drew back in my mind. It was almost a physical sensation. Changes occurred in my brain, like hundreds of dominoes falling over at the same time. Topple, crash, the confusion was gone with a new dark reality taking its place. I stood up and walked away from Rob, and sat on a bench by the sea. I still didn't know who I was but I knew what I was, I was worthless; a nothing. The crashing certainty of it all swamped me.

I sat on the bench for ten hours without moving. At first, Rob tried to talk me into moving, he sounded worried, then he went to the club and got Abigail, who tried to get me to go back to the apartment. To her absolute credit, Abigail stayed with me for the full ten hours, saying different things to try and get me to move. I'm sorry for that, it must have been horrible for her. I didn't go to the toilet, eat or drink; I sat and watched the sun come up, while the night-time people left looking tired and the daytime people arrived looking freshly washed and dressed, smelling of suntan lotion and coffee.

I find it hard to explain what happened next. I stood up and ran away from my friend, feeling all ties with the world go. It was a beautiful sunny afternoon and I headed away from the strip and up the mountain in the vague direction of our apartment. I didn't turn off towards where I thought the apartment was but carried on into unknown territory. I stopped on a ledge and surveyed my surroundings, glad Abigail was still some way off. It was peaceful, the magnificent beauty of the sun on my face and arms was soothing. Somewhere nearby, cars zoomed up a road. The sea sparkled in the distance. Everything seemed vivid, so technicolour perfect. I ran faster, trying to get away from my friend, desperately wanting to be alone. Not concentrating on what I was doing, I ran too close to the edge, slipped, and fell a long way. Everything was hushed; I was relaxed. I thought: I want to live. Then blackness.

Chapter Two

Leaving My Body

There was a zooming sensation then I popped back into my head. Wow, I thought. Wow, wow, wow. I'm OK, I'm alive! This is great, I wanted to live and here I am. This is one of the best days ever. Exhilaration and joy filled me to the brim, because not only was I alive, I felt fantastic, awesome, amazing. I felt so great, I couldn't remember ever feeling better. I knew there was a contrast between how I felt then and how I'd felt at the club, but other than acknowledging the difference in feelings, I knew I didn't need to dwell on it any further.

Hang on, I thought. I'm actually hovering around the area where my head is, instead of actually being inside my head. Now I *know* how crazy this sounds to most people. Believe me, if anyone had told me something like this before it happened to me, I would have presumed they were either hallucinating, dreaming, crazy or something else, rather than accept that they were actually hovering around their own head. However, it really happened to me and all I can do is tell the truth.

Being able to go away from my head didn't bother me; it felt like an extremely normal thing to do. I felt like myself, the essence of me, in a way I hadn't done for years, possibly ever. Because I felt so myself and comfortable, there was nothing to fear, because if I was me away from my body then what was there to be scared of?

Everything felt perfect and I felt contented, enjoying the experience of being wrapped in a warm, invisible blanket of comfort. Delicious peace coursed through me. I was aware that I could hear everything going on around me in microscopic detail.

There was crunching on the concrete, sirens, wheels stopping in a gravelly way. Men's voices talking very fast. I hummed to myself, enjoying it all. I still hovered around the area where my head was but I knew I could move away from it if I wanted, because I'd done this. However, I wasn't ready to move too far away.

I thought it was hilarious that everyone was making such a fuss. I wanted to tell them to relax, that I felt absolutely great and not to worry. Instead I just accepted my tranquil state and enjoyed listening.

At some point I became aware that there was a weird grating sound in my ear. It wasn't exactly annoying but I did wonder when it was going to stop.

I developed an awareness of a soothing, pearly, bright light right in front of me. At first I presumed that I was looking at the sunlight. There was no feeling that because I was away from my head I should no longer be able to see. While being a hundred per cent aware of the two-part stretcher being pushed underneath my body from both sides in order to meet in the middle, I also became absorbed in the light. I didn't go into it, I just stared at it, feeling surrounded by absolute peace and love. It seemed so obvious then how loved I was, it seemed a bit silly to have ever felt unloved.

I know who I am, I thought. I KNOW WHO I AM. I'm me! It's so obvious, why has it taken this long for it to click? I am me, Hannah, to my core and beyond. I love being me.

Everything just felt so right, so perfect. I could think with a clarity I couldn't remember experiencing before, but there was no need to plan and over think. Everything was absolutely fine just as it was.

Something was fitted round my neck, then I was lifted up and slid into the back of the ambulance, then we set off to the hospital.

As well as being able to go out of my head I was also able to go downwards and on several occasions sank through my body, weird as that may sound. I was aware of the light the whole time. My purpose, which was extremely fun and relaxing, became to look at the light; I felt drawn to it. I *really* liked that light.

At the hospital there was a flurry of activity. I was pushed down corridors, enjoying listening to everything and feeling peaceful.

There was a humour in the peace, I felt uplifted and happy. We arrived in a room, then we went to another place for X-rays and my head was put in a tunnel thing. Someone rapped at the door, I was wheeled off. I didn't like some of the things being done to me so purposefully stayed out of my head more and more. Clatter, noise, fast voices, machines.

A doctor cut my top in half, it was my friend's top that I'd borrowed and I wondered if she'd be annoyed. I gave the light in front of me my full attention. I was aware of a pulling sensation around my belly button and I was drawn upwards out of my body. It was blissful and I was happy to go, I'd never felt better; I was bursting with peace, joy and love. I went up and a little bit away from my body in the light but at that moment a female doctor started patting my hand really hard and shouting,

"Hannah!" in a Spanish accent.

I tried to ignore her. I knew what was happening; I was dying and she was trying to bring me back. By then I was hooked up to several monitors and I presume that at that point the medical staff could see a change. Because dying no longer equalled what I'd previously thought it did but instead was about feeling more amazing and loved than I ever had before, I was happy to carry on with it. The doctor, however, was not pleased with this course of action and she kept whacking my hand and shouting my name.

I went back down feeling inexplicably disappointed. In some ways I don't really feel I had a choice in this. I'd wanted to carry on going upwards really badly. I had this overwhelming feeling that it was time to open my eyes. I fought it, I really didn't want to open my eyes, my current state was fine. But for some reason I knew now was the time to open my eyes, it really was and I had to get on with it.

I opened my eyes.

Chapter Three

Hospital

I looked around for the light. Where had it gone? The only lights were electric ones which looked dull and yellow in comparison. I felt confused about where the light was for a while.

A woman doctor spoke to me fast in Spanish and broken English; she was telling me I was going to be taken somewhere else. There were lots of medical staff in the room, attaching tubes and pouches. Oh, I thought. Maybe this is more serious than I thought.

Really annoyingly, all the calm feelings of utter peace and love began to dissipate as I took in the scene around me. It looked like something from *Casualty* or *ER*. I remember clarity turning to confusion as I wondered where the other feelings had gone. I'd felt so great, why had that dissolved? I couldn't move, I could only move my eyes, feet, one arm and hands. My body, neck and other arm felt completely stuck, paralysed. Panic flooded everything. I wanted to get the peace back.

I was wheeled out of the room, down the corridor, put in the back of an ambulance and taken to a larger hospital. It was an exceptionally rattly ride, even though I was firmly strapped to a stretcher on a gurney, and it seemed to take years. Every atom and particle in my body felt like it was being thoroughly shaken during each moment of the journey. I'm sure it was just a normal drive but for some reason that shaking and rattling sensation has always stayed with me; I can even feel it now as I write.

I remember being pushed into the emergency room in the new hospital. All the hospital notes I have from Tenerife are from this second hospital, Complejo Hospitalario Nuestra Senora Candelaria, and the recorded time of arrival is in the early hours of the 1st February 1998. I wish I had my notes from the first hospital but have been unable to get them. I was awake when we arrived, several staff were there and a nice lady asked me questions in Spanish with lots of miming, like, was I pregnant? They did an ultrasound just to make sure; definitely not.

Soon after I arrived I became unable to breathe; it felt like all the air had been sucked out of my lungs. Suddenly a river of blood shot out of my mouth and kept coming, quickly turning the sheet covering me red. I massively panicked. Even though a short time before I'd left my body and was quite happy to continue with that course of action, in the physical world, where I'd become instantly immersed in my own life and surroundings, blood plus no ability to breathe had equalled panic and a huge desire to breathe again. A doctor with curly hair came round to my right side and pushed a tube though my ribs and into my lung to drain out the blood; his actions were so precise, perfect and competent. I could breathe again, one of the most amazing, beautiful sensations I can remember. I've always felt indebted to that doctor. Looking back, I find it amazing that everything that happened did so with the view to me staying alive. If my lung had become flooded with blood seconds after I fell or even in either of the ambulances, would I have survived? I was in the right place at the right time for it to be treated.

Pain kicked in with intent. My body felt like a cage with me fitted wrongly inside it. The pain was a vibration so intense that it almost numbed itself. I became aware that my ears, eyes and nose were oozing blood. Strangely, my fingernails were fine, not even a scratch.

Someone tried to shove a tube down my throat. For some reason this enraged me, it had been a long day and it's a very undignified (but obviously worthwhile) procedure, so I grabbed it and tried to swallow it myself. Having a tiny bit of control over the proceedings helped. I gagged at first but managed it on about the fourth attempt. There. Done.

All of a sudden I felt overwhelmingly dehydrated. The most

important thing in the world became having a drink, I went almost mad trying to mime "water". The doctor with the curly hair initially shook his head but in the end he allowed a nurse to wet my lips with a sponge, the best drink I've ever had. I wanted her to do it more and more although she couldn't because the doctor wouldn't let her.

I noticed that the arm I couldn't move was bending the wrong way and that there was a hole at the elbow with a piece of bone sticking out of it. I showed the doctor with the curly hair. "Don't worry about it," he mimed. It stayed like that for over six days.

We all stayed in the emergency room for a while longer, then when the doctors were happy I'd stabilized enough, we caught a lift up to the intensive care unit. I was pushed into a kind of cubicle space. It was the middle of the night, there was pitch black outside my window.

At that point I passed out into the deepest sleep of my life. I dreamed I whizzed down a tunnel and ended up in a relaxed waiting room like the lounge at the airport. I know the analogies are obvious so won't go into them. There were three of us sitting on a corner sofa, with me in the middle. I don't remember what the other two looked like but they were very nice. There was a conversation, with the upshot being that I was going to stay and that everything was OK. It was definitely a dream, it wasn't like the NDE, but it was exceptionally clear and vivid.

I woke up the next morning with sunlight on my face. This made me unbelievably happy; I suddenly understood how beautiful sunlight was, it felt so fresh and alive, so tangible and real. At the same time, amid the morphine, I felt sad and strange. I only had to feel and look at the state of my body to see how far I'd fallen, literally. The near-death experience was very much with me, although I had no idea what it was at that stage, I'd never heard of NDEs before, and I longed to feel that good about myself again and to be immersed in utter peace. But the fact was, it was time to face reality. I felt hungry to be alive and the sense that I'd been given a chance to start over was dawning on me but it was more than evident that the journey was going to be painful.

The nurses were like angels, coming in and out, adjusting drips, adding new bags of blood (I needed many blood transfusions), checking the vast array of equipment attached to me. Luckily thirst was no longer a problem; I was being fed and watered intravenously. I couldn't open my jaw wider than about a centimetre and the general pain all over my body had become a hideous, permanent presence, dulled by the morphine but not taken away. I was on a water mattress and at one point a nurse accidentally nudged the end of it by mistake when she was walking past. Unbelievably strong ripples of pain ricocheted through my body making me scream out. I still had no idea what my injuries were, although the arm one was pretty obvious and my vision was very strange, being wonky and distorted. I was having a hard time understanding exactly what had happened. I'd come to Tenerife for a holiday, admittedly in a pretty run-down state, and ended up mashed up in intensive care. How and why? I felt embarrassed about it, but all the time a teeming drive to get better and live was flooding my system.

A doctor came to talk to me. He wanted to explain my injuries, and as I couldn't speak Spanish and he couldn't speak English we started a long pantomime of miming and saying things slowly and loudly in our own languages. I didn't really understand much of what he was trying to say, other than that I had skull fractures and a broken pelvis. The bone was still sticking out of my arm but he indicated it would stay like that until they thought I was stable enough to operate on. My hospital notes "6 de Febrero de 1998" explain that I have to wait for arm surgery, "La paciente queda pendiente de intervencion quiurgica en brazo dcho... A su alta porta drenaje pleural dcho. Aun permeable." My lung had collapsed the day before but he was trying to explain other injuries too. In the end we gave up and he said my parents had been informed and would be arriving the next day. This threw me into a quandary, I'd never seen both my parents in the same room together, it would be too weird if they both turned up together. The doctor also said my friend, Abigail, was OK but shocked, and was flying back to the UK to be with her family; I felt very sorry she'd had to go through all that and desperately hoped she was OK.

As soon as I knew my mother was on her way every second seemed like a year. I wanted her to arrive right then and there; the waiting was torture. I got very upset that afternoon and a nurse came and held my hand for ages. It was a dramatic lesson in the power of touch and compassion, the simple act of her holding my hand made me feel physically and psychologically different and better in an instant.

Being awake for more than half an hour was tiring and I continually dropped off into deep sleeps throughout the day and night. Nurses and doctors bustled in and out, they were all so kind and I will always feel indebted to them.

The next day my mother arrived. Thankfully she was with my godfather, Peter, and not my father. She looked shell-shocked as she'd been told to prepare herself for anything but she said later that as soon as she saw my one working eye she knew I'd be OK. Apparently it was very alive, although bruised. The other eye was pretty much stuck together. The doctor came back to explain my injuries to her but the language barrier was still a problem and they didn't get very far. A man, who the doctors later said they didn't know, stopped my mother in the corridor and asked if she wanted him to translate everything for her. She readily accepted his offer and he came with her for a meeting with the doctor and patiently translated everything that was said. Then he walked off and no one ever saw him again. Before the accident I had become disillusioned about religion and spirituality and was sceptical about the concept of angels, but so many things happened around this time to challenge my views that now I think very differently. Whether this man was an angel or a translator who the doctors had never met or a kind person who could read situations well, we'll never know, but he really helped my mother that day, which I'll always be very grateful for.

My mother explained that I had three skull fractures and internal bleeding in my head, a pneumothorax and right pulmonary contusion that was now improving thanks to the chest drain, liver trauma, three pelvic fractures and a broken arm. Or as it says in my hospital notes, "Neumotorax Y Contusion Pulmonar Derecha, Traumatismo Hepatico, Fractura Iliopubiana Bilateral E Isquiopubiana Izquierda, Fractura Temporal Derecha, Paralisis De Vi Par Derecho, Fractura De Olecranon Derecha." The liver trauma was the worst, and they wouldn't operate on my arm until it had improved, in case I died during the operation. My vision was strange because my right eye had become stuck staring to the left, caused by the sixth cranial nerve becoming paralysed. The fact that my eye was stuck to the left worried me more than all the other injuries put together, how vain!

My mum wasn't allowed to stay for long so she and my godfather went back to their hotel. I fell asleep as soon as she left, ridiculously tired out after their visit but enormously happy they'd come. I was in the ICU for five days and my mum came to visit me every day, my godfather travelling home after a couple of days. Being there, unable to move or feed myself, gave me much time for thought, morphine tinged as it was. I had a new lust for life; I now knew I wanted to get a university place and study. I also couldn't remember how to be the me that I was before my accident, which isn't surprising really given that I'd been having an identity crisis, but it felt like I was a blank canvas, not a worthless robot, who now had hope and possibilities.

I wanted to heal and get home as soon as possible, impatience is still something I need to work on every day, and was very happy when I was allowed to graduate from the ICU to my own room on a lower floor; by then I could open my mouth wider and my injuries had begun to heal. My notes from that day say, "Consciente, orientada, no habla castellano." I was conscious, orientated and did not speak Castilian. The hospital staff dragged another bed into the room for my mum and she moved into hospital too for the remainder of my stay. Our relationship was already healing and continued to do so in Tenerife; we've been extremely close ever since. The room was spick and span and smelt of sunshine and cleaning products – apparently north Tenerife, where the hospital was, has a subtropical hot climate but is usually cloudier and wetter than south Tenerife.[13] I had the opposite experience – our days in Playa de las Américas were overcast and breezy, whereas warm sunlight burst through the hospital window every day.

The next day a doctor from the UK flew out. I'd taken out travel insurance and luckily his services were covered by that. He had a meeting with all the consultants I was under and they explained that my liver was still too damaged to cope with an aeroplane flight so they asked him to come back a week later. I was distraught when he explained this, having become fixated on returning to the UK, but that was that.

I had two nightmares at this point, both of which were horrifyingly real. During one I was buried alive under the ground, packed in with earth and worms, screaming to be let out but never being rescued. It was claustrophobic and terrifying. In the second I was climbing dark stairs in a seedy club. An atmosphere of evil permeated everything; there was a door I had to walk towards and behind it I knew unspeakably evil acts were being committed. If I went through that door I would become part of the evil. I tried to get away but for some reason I couldn't stop walking down the corridor towards the door. At that point I woke up. These nightmares were so vivid, they seemed to be more than just dreams. Fear-filled, perhaps? A warning not to go back to old ways?

At some point around that time, I tried to explain to my mother how I'd left my body immediately after the accident, and I described everything the paramedics and doctors had done, all the X-rays I'd had while in this other state. My mum tried her best to understand what I was saying, but I don't think either of us really knew what to make of it. The day-to-day realities of pain and injuries took precedence, although I thought about the experience of being away from my body each day, yearning for those wonderful feelings of peace and love to come back. The whole thing had felt so normal and natural and fantastic that it didn't seem like something to make a fuss about; it also felt like a very private experience that I didn't want tainted by doubt, so I decided not to mention it to any of the medical staff. I was also aware that perhaps I wasn't in the best state to start making statements about consciousness leaving the body; everyone knew I'd been out all night before the accident and I thought they'd put it down to me being either delusional or having hallucinations. I suppose that by not telling them I was partly protecting myself, I didn't want to come across as crazy. Or perhaps more accurately, crazier than I already did.

Small breakthroughs started happening. Having my hair washed for the first time since the accident was fabulous. It was full of dried blood and completely stuck together, and a nurse brought a bowl and shampoo and attempted to wash as much as she could. I still couldn't lift my head but she did a great job and got most of my hair. Another breakthrough was having tubes removed and being allowed to drink through a straw, then one day being given my first meal. A nurse brought me a tray with meat and potatoes on it and indicated that I shouldn't eat too much, but I ate the whole lot, the best meal of my life!

The long, wide windowsill in our room filled up with huge bunches of flowers and cards sent from relatives and friends in the UK. I remembered the love I'd felt during the NDE. The messages, cards and flowers made me realise how many people actually cared about me and I was genuinely shocked; every emotion felt was raw and real, it was a real eye-opener. I realised how much I loved all of them. I was really glad that almost as many messages of support came for my mother; the guilt I felt at putting her through this was immense.

The doctor from the UK flew back a week later and this time successfully escorted me all the way to King's College Hospital. Arriving at Heathrow felt very much like coming home. I loved being able to speak the same language as everyone again. I really appreciated that. The two paramedics who lifted my stretcher off the plane were so kind and relaxed, full of humour and cracking jokes. I noticed kindness around me all the time. I'm sure kindness had been around me all my life but I never really *saw* and understood it until after the accident.

I loved being given a bed on a long, old-fashioned ward in King's College Hospital. In a way, it reminded me of being in a dormitory at school, everybody in the same boat, calling out to each other across the room. The atmosphere was different here; a lot more relaxed than in Tenerife.

It must have been nice for my mum to go home and sleep in her own bed that night. She'd been an absolute rock throughout her whole stay in Tenerife and now she was exhausted. Our neighbours came and picked her up, took her home and made her dinner. I didn't sleep much that night. My notes from King's College Hospital record that at 10:00pm on 14/2/98 I was "admitted to ward accompanied by mum and a Dr from a hospital in Tenerife." As well as the previously documented injuries they recorded "multiple bruising".

My mother contacted my father at this time, to tell him what happened.

He replied in March 1998.

Dear Emma,
It's been a dreadful business for Hannah. I hope very much that things have been moving in the right direction, medically and all round, with help available, and will continue thus.

A nice sentiment, he didn't feel the need to visit. I found my feelings and perception about the situation with him going through new and different stages from then on.

My mother, possibly at her wits end at such a stressful time and sick of dealing with parenting by herself, wrote to a cardinal around now to tell him what was going on. To me, this seems like a cry for help.

One of his replies to this letter is dated March 1998.

Dear Emma,

I was very sad to realise that my letter sent to you in Santa Cruz has never reached you. It was faxed on 6 February and the fax machine confirmed that it had been received. I am enclosing the letter for you now.

I would ask you to approach Hannah's father directly yourself and tell him that I know. I will then impress on him how he must take on his responsibilities in this matter.

With kindest regards…

This letter must have shone out as a ray of hope for my mother. At last someone – a cardinal no less – was going to help James accept more parental responsibility. When she told me about this, I – still thinking my father had normal human responses like guilt to situations – became worried and asked her to tell the Cardinal to be very careful with my father, in case he felt so guilty at being found out that he harmed himself. In hindsight I can see how foolishly ignorant I was at this stage about his true nature. The Cardinal got in touch with Michael Jamison at my mother's suggestion, because he'd been involved as a mediator all along. He then wrote this letter to my mother in March 1998:

Dear Emma,

I have been in touch with Michael Jamison, as you suggested.

I have had a long talk with him and he is going to tell the priest to come and see me. He is going to tell him that I am aware (without

saying how) of his situation. Michael is going to tell him that it is time
that he came and discussed the whole situation with me personally. I
think that this is a satisfactory step which we can now take.

With kindest regards.

Yours sincerely…

So proceedings are still sounding positive, the Cardinal is taking responsibility and has asked James to meet with him. My mother must have been excited, perhaps feeling that this was going to be the breakthrough meeting that she'd been hoping for years, which would spark James into having fatherly feelings and perhaps into apologising for not wanting to meet me until I was fourteen years old.

At some point, soon after this, my father and the Cardinal met. During this meeting, my father used his persuasive powers to convince the Cardinal that he was in fact a good father under the circumstances and had done everything possible to look after his hedonistic, wayward daughter and to support her mother. He produced copies of letters, lists of money sent, recounted meetings with me and showed willing to meet with Michael Jamison to continue talking about what was best to do. After this meeting, the Cardinal's letters to my mother adopted a different tone. I will discuss these in more detail later on.

Around this time, full of my newfound zest for life (from my hospital bed) I started to see matters to do with my father in a new light. Instead of feeling cowed, like I was a shameful secret that should be hidden away from the world forever, I became idealistic, full of newly discovered zeal. It suddenly seemed obvious that James was a hypocrite, and should leave the priesthood. I felt angry and righteous. How could he maintain an identity of a chaste, hardworking Catholic priest when he'd made selfish choices throughout his life, always putting his own needs before his daughter's? How would his congregation feel if they knew the truth? He must leave, I decided, it was the only way forward. My thoughts must have been communicated to the Cardinal, as he wrote this letter back in June 1998:

Dear Emma,

Thank you for your letter. I suggested that you should go and see Dr Michael Jamison because we have reached an impasse. I thought it might help to have the professional opinions of someone who knows the parties involved. We have reached an impasse because you appear to be convinced that the only way forward for Hannah is that James should leave the priesthood. I am not convinced this is so.

With kindest regards,

Yours sincerely…

I have a letter dated June 1998, from Michael Jamison that echoes these thoughts:

Dear Emma,

Thank you very much for your letter. It is true that the Cardinal has written to me about the ongoing situation. He has not clarified specifically what he wants me to do. He is unhappy about the suggestion that James should leave the priesthood, but perhaps you should write to the Cardinal and ask for clarification of what he wants you to discuss with me. It is no good coming to see me if you are not happy about the visit and if you are not sure what you want to discuss.

Yours sincerely,

M. Jamison, Consultant Psychiatrist

I find this letter very interesting because for me it points to a change in attitude towards my mother. Michael Jamison says that the Cardinal "has not clarified specifically what he wants me to do." Suddenly Michael Jamison does not come across as an impartial mediator between two people, he is now beholden to a higher power who can tell him what to do. If this is the case, how can he be unbiased? He goes on to issue a reprimand, "It is no good coming to see me if you are not happy about the visit and if you are not sure what you want to discuss." This sounds like a parent talking to a petulant child. I feel frustrated on behalf of my mother, having to wade through constant setbacks all the time.

From time to time, while writing this book and reading through all the letters from the priests and Michael Jamison, I have felt cowed again, like I did when I was younger. I can totally see their point of view, I have understood it and been part of it for years and sometimes it overtakes me and I think it's real. They think it's real and they utterly believe that everything they've said and done is alright. But if this is so, why does everything to do with him make me feel awful? During one moment of feeling cowed and insignificant in a world of powerful men, I contacted Coping International, an organisation recently set up to help the children of priests. "He's done all this," I explained, listing everything. "Does this mean he's a good father under the circumstances? Do you have a perspective on this?" "Yes," came their reply. "It's called bribery without love." Ah.

My hospital notes from King's state that on 19th February 1998 I "mobilised bed to chair. Fully weight bearing on left leg. Partial weight bearing on right leg." Then the next day, "Mobilising with gutter rollator frame," then day after that, "Mobilising to and from toilet with crutches," then two days later, "Walking well with x2 crutches – to do stairs later, sutures from chest drain and elbow removed." Everyone was kind in King's and I enjoyed the more relaxed atmosphere but I just wanted to get home. Various scans were always getting lost and on 25th February my notes state, "Unfortunately CT head not in packet, is not reported on, will continue to chase this." Me being discharged hinged on the doctor reviewing this scan as they thought they'd found another skull fracture and wanted to check it. On 26th February 1998 my notes state that I was: "Wanting to see if films were back. Explained they weren't but that I was trying to track doctor down. I will try to find him again this afternoon. Explained we are not happy to let her go unless CT has excluded a depressed skull fracture. She says she will self-discharge at 5pm if films are not found." Wow, a classic illustration of my impatience problems. Later on 26th February the notes state, "CT could not find scan. Hannah wanted to self-discharge. CT said they would print out copies of the film. The doctor then wasn't in the department. Another doctor reported on them – provisional report. Slightly depressed temporal fracture. No subdural... doctor is happy for Hannah to go home in view of provisional CT report." Hurray! So I was discharged, twenty-six days after being admitted to hospital in Tenerife.

Chapter Four

Recovery

I feel I should emphasise, at this point, that before the accident I'd become very sceptical and disillusioned about religion and spirituality. I didn't see the two as different, I thought of both religion and spirituality as pretty much the same thing and wasn't impressed by either. My father being a priest who preached about love but was unable to put this love into practice struck me as hypocritical and corrupt, and tainted my view of the Catholic Church in general. Before my accident I couldn't honestly see how life could go on after death, there was no proof of it, it just seemed like another lie peddled by the Church.

After the accident, however, when I'd actually experienced leaving my body and had a glimpse into a fresh new state of being, one that involved being surrounded by peace and love while enjoying a crystal clear clarity of thought and feeling, I felt very different about spirituality. My consciousness, me, had left my body, and I'd still existed. In fact I'd felt better than ever. It had been very real, natural and normal. So what did that mean? The near-death experience threw all my previous beliefs out of the window and opened up many new channels of thought, while allowing in a multitude of questions. Later on, looking back, it seemed as though at that moment – when I'd separated from my body and experienced life away from it, brief though it was – I was being given the most important jigsaw piece in the puzzle of my life, the one that would eventually help me piece all the other bits together until one day I would have an overview of the bigger picture.

In King's College Hospital I'd had moments of euphoria, the memories of my clear state of mind still fresh, the feeling of being surrounded by love and peace still easy to bring back. On one level, life made so much more sense, but on another, it had become very confusing. As well as the good feelings I felt horror about the actual accident and injuries, guilt and shame for putting my mother through what had happened, trepidation at the months of recovery that obviously lay ahead and confusion at how my former life had been wiped away. But the love I was shown by friends and family was affirming and overwhelming; it carried me through those days in hospital. I had an endless stream of visitors, friends from my past and present, relatives and friends of my mothers, who came on a daily basis, supporting both me and my mum, bringing lovely gifts of homemade scones, flowers, chocolates, cards, unexpected exciting presents, and on one occasion two cheeseburgers from McDonald's that I'd asked a friend to smuggle in. At that point I was living in the moment, still with adrenalin coursing through me, my thoughts fragmented and the experiences completely unintegrated, but I was OK from day to day.

A few days after I got back to my mother's flat, a blisteringly awful depression crashed over me, and stayed for several months. The reality of leaving my body and the NDE were in no way erased or forgotten during this time; I think they'd just been temporarily pushed to the side so I could try to come to terms with the horror, shame and guilt of what had happened. Also, I've since learned that depression is one of the most common conditions following trauma. In 1999, the Trauma Recovery Project found that there is a:

> prolonged and profound level of functional limitation after major trauma at 12-month and 18-month follow-up. This is the first report of long-term outcome based on the QWB Scale, a standardized quality-of-life measure, and provides new and provocative evidence that the magnitude of dysfunction after major injury has been underestimated. Postinjury depression, PTSD, serious extremity injury, and intensive care unit days are significantly associated with 12-month and 18-month QWB outcome.[14]

In fact during that first year I was diagnosed with post-traumatic stress disorder (PTSD), and chose to join a research programme at the Centre for Anxiety Disorders and Trauma in Denmark Hill, London, where I received free trauma counselling in exchange for my response being used in research. The consultant psychotherapist who worked with me was so compassionate that I found just his attitude healing, not to mention the techniques he used to try and help me integrate what had happened. The counselling model he used was cognitive and behavioural, and I found the whole experience very useful; it definitely helped my recovery along. I trusted him enough to explain that on several occasions I'd left my body and he said, "Ah, a classic case of dissociation. It's common for people to feel as though they have left their bodies during a particularly traumatic event, but they are not really leaving their bodies, they are protecting themselves with a great defence mechanism." Tara Brach supports this point, saying:

> In order to make it through such sudden and severe pain, victims of trauma typically dissociate from their bodies... Some people feel "unreal," as if they have left their body and are experiencing life from a great distance. They do whatever they can to keep from feeling the raw sensations of fear and pain in their body.[15]

I really liked my therapist, even though he was a man and I still had the feeling that men wouldn't treat me very well, so I didn't press my case, but I secretly knew that I had left my body and it hadn't just been dissociation.

Around this time, after his meeting with my father, the Cardinal wrote a letter to my mother. It had a very different tone to his previous ones and although I'm not in possession of it I can tell from her reply, which I do have a copy of, that it referred to a statement by Frank Harding, accused her of having a relationship with a priest in 1977, stated that wrong decisions were made during the meeting of 1977 and accused me of being a dissolute individual.

My mother's reply dated May 1998, which I've quoted part of earlier in the book, reads as follows:

Dear Cardinal,

Thank you for your letter. My own position will hopefully be clarified through the following points:

In your letter you say I had a relationship with a priest in 1977. James Carson was not a priest or even a deacon then. He was on a shortened course for mature candidates. His behaviour in his relationship with me was not priestly at any time.

With reference to another of your points, I agree that with hindsight the decisions taken were wrong. At the time I felt them to be wrong. Never at any time did I think James should go forward into the priesthood given the circumstances and his nature.

Please take the following points very seriously:

In 1977, James never discussed with me on my own what we should do. All his discussions seemed to be with Father Harding. I never knew what was said in these.

I knew I was pregnant from April 1977. From April until after his exams in June, I agreed that he could study and we would wait until after that to discuss what should be done. He refused to discuss it with me when the time came.

I was unaware, at that time, of the extent of his friendship with Father Harding. He insisted that I come to "have a short chat" with Father Harding. I did not want to do this. I thought we should be sorting it out ourselves but I went as he was so insistent.

The chat turned out to be a meeting to which James came to fully prepared with several sheets of A4 paper containing his choices, totally undiscussed with me.

I had no idea that this was the meeting where a final and conclusive decision was to be made. In no way was I ready for that. I had been in a state of shock and bewilderment since finding out I was pregnant. I could not understand why James would not discuss the situation with me.

He started the meeting by saying, "Of course marriage is out of the question," (his words). This had never previously been discussed.

The only choice I wanted was that we should wait until after the baby was born until any decision was made. This was rejected immediately without discussion as he said he had a date for his ordination.

James was looking for black and white answers in a situation that had none and in which rushed decisions could not be made.

I was not being listened to, and it suddenly became obvious to me that since April he had been desperately extricating himself out of any responsibility. By this point I was too hurt to listen any more.

He went on reading from his notes. All the choices were his. He had no right then and has no right now to say that any part of the decision was mine. Such a decision only he could make and through his neglectful and cowardly actions through the previous months he had in practice already made it.

How dare he then try to foist on to me the responsibility for making his decision for him about how he was going to respond to his baby? I had already made my decision about my own response.

Regarding the "statement" of Frank Harding, I cannot see what influence on the situation such a statement, written twenty years after the event by a third party, can have on decisions that may be made now or in the future. Legally it would bear very little weight.

My own thoughts are that Hannah's request that her father is laicized is because she believes it is wrong that he is still a priest, whilst living a lie. She presumed that the hierarchy would agree with this. The ideals of young people are very real.

The church either objectively sees the situation as wrong, or, in allowing him to continue, condones the lie, the hypocrisy and the scandalizing of his daughter... James stated several times (in writing too) that if the Cardinal knew, then he would have to leave. If he is consistent in what he says he should be in process of leaving now.

At this point I would like to say I appreciate the efforts you made *earlier in attempting to initiate a healthy process between Hannah and James. I'm sorry it didn't work. I had spent fifteen years hoping for this and quietly and regularly attempting to make him realise the importance of building up a relationship with Hannah.*

It was not the becoming a priest that was so wrong (though I think it was wrong) but the way he handled his relationship with his daughter over these twenty years that was so gravely wounding.

He treated with contempt any suggestions I made, right up until recently, when I warned him not to mention the need for secrecy to Hannah. Instead he reiterated the necessity for secrecy on every occasion and even mentioned it on the only birthday card he's ever sent her.

Because I so single-mindedly pursued the idea of reconciliation between Hannah and James I did not consider disturbing his way of life as a priest, the two would have been in conflict and to my mind building a relationship with his daughter was far more important.

At the meeting in 1977 I watched Frank Harding and James Carson – a priest and a trainee – glibly preparing to lie by omission. I found it extraordinary and dis-edifying. I have never publicised the situation nor ever lied about it but I felt that they were wrong.

It was also their responsibility to tell you. At that time I presumed they had let you know. I knew nothing about the machinery of the secular priesthood then and have tried not to know too much about it since.

Hannah sees a counsellor for post traumatic stress. Her accident was enormous and devastating... I would appreciate it if you would change your term in the church records... [Most teenagers sic] get away on the whole without being labelled... I feel that writing things like this into official records makes it more difficult for her. [My thoughts were] told to you in what I thought was an atmosphere of confidentiality. So I am surprised and distressed that it is written into what I have to presume is an official record.

Also points nine and ten. Things I said at the end of our meeting after a particularly difficult week. My anxiety level was high and I was feeling intensely anxious about Hannah's well-being. I was not trying to imply anything about your being to blame. I said it in exhaustion, hoping for reassurance. I'm sorry I said it as it was open to misinterpretation. This week Hannah is much better and more hopeful. Had she read your letter it would have caused her great distress.

Because you made points eight, nine and ten I have to presume now that there will be no more speaking in confidence to you… I will consider getting in touch with Michael Jamison.

With best wishes,

Yours sincerely,

Emma

It seems like an abrupt end to what had previously looked like a potentially supportive and constructive relationship with the Cardinal. My mother had clearly gained confidence in speaking out, or no longer cared about the consequences, and was trying to clearly put her own case across. It must have been so hard looking after me in 1998 by herself, I think she just wanted some help and support. Not just words in the odd letter, but support that actually counted. Her continual fight for a relationship between my father and I is truly remarkable.

It seems that the concept of me being a hedonistic, degenerate teenager had really bothered the Cardinal. Did I live through the best part of the 1990s (up until the end of January 1998) in the midst of a party lifestyle? Yes I most certainly did, pretty much like most of the other teenagers I knew at the time! I was a rebellious teenager; a complete nightmare in fact! But since my accident I just want to get the most out of life, and try and make life OK for people around me. I still often get things wrong, but I now know that's all part of the journey; and if you act from a place of love and kindness as often as you can, you can't go too off course.

When I expressed my fears about the Church painting me as a dissolute individual to Coping International if I ever "broke my silence", their response made me laugh and feel slightly less scared: "Oh my God... you mean... you were a teenager?...You are DEFINITELY the first... Wouldn't any discerning adult ask the question (after hearing my story) 'Were we her parents?'" Well when you put it like that...

As the depression lifted, I began to have a tangible sense of 'moving forward' in life. Not physically forward, as although my injuries had healed and I could walk normally (although my eyesight was still distorted) I became tired ridiculously easily and tried to limit going anywhere to once or twice a week. I felt that things were changing. I wanted to learn – ultimately I wanted to understand what went on in people's minds (and my own); unravel the layers of their psychology and consciousness perhaps. But I knew then that I wasn't at the right stage for that as my own thoughts were still being jumbled and all over the place; I had a new, raw appreciation of life but was still getting flashbacks of the accident every day and nightmares most nights. I had a sense that if I was patient, studying psychology in some form would come later.

I applied to the University of Reading to read history of art and was accepted, being given a place to start in September 1999. This gave a satisfying sense of triumph. In November 1998 I started an evening course run by Birkbeck College (part of the University of London) called "The Foundations of Modern Psychology".

I was so glad when New Year's Eve finally arrived at the end of 1998. I went to a friend's house and we had a quiet but happy celebration; never before had I been so pleased to see the back of the old year and the beginning of the new. It really did feel like a fresh start, a clean slate; a whole new year in which to start living to the full.

Then in July 1999, something unexpected happened.

My cousin and I went to stay by the seaside. Our grandparents had lived in Worthing, Sussex, and we had good, shared memories of staying there when we were little, playing on the shingly beach, floating out to sea in giant rubber rings and playing at the park. We decided to go back for a night, staying at a B&B along the seafront. We went out for a meal, chatted continuously, had a few drinks then returned to our B&B and fell asleep.

In the middle of the night I woke up, or was woken up, I'm not really sure which, by a figure surrounded by a bluish light at the end of my bed. It was a woman and she had a kind, compassionate atmosphere around her. She kept communicating to me that I needed to take my mother to hospital. I'd had a few glasses of wine that evening so was trying to work out whether this woman was really there or whether I'd invented her. I think I indicated that I'd taken her message on board, then fell back to sleep. The next morning my cousin drove me home, and later that day I found my mother curled up on her bed looking as ill as it's possible for a human to look while still being alive. Fear took me over and in a confusion, perhaps directed by the vision or dream I'd had, or perhaps just because she was grey and ill looking, I asked the lady who lived in the flat above us to drive my mother and I to hospital as I still hadn't passed my driving test. My mother was so ill she couldn't sit on a chair in the waiting room at the hospital and lay down across several chairs. She was soon admitted and after many investigations I was told she had cancer and would need an operation immediately.

In the months before this happened, my mum had been suffering from terrible abdominal cramps. She'd been to the doctor several times, who patiently explained to her that all she had was indigestion. The doctors at the hospital, however, found a massive tumour in her intestine and scheduled an operation immediately. I found it much more painful to be the well person who's willing the ill person to get better than being the sick person in hospital; your will for the other person to get better is so strong it's physically painful, coupled with the worry at possible outcomes, the realisation about how much you love that person and aren't ready for them to leave you yet. Although I'd had a spiritual experience myself, leaving my body during the NDE, I hadn't yet integrated it into my life; all my energy had so far gone on healing. I knew my mother would be fine if she died; but we'd been through so much and were closer than ever, it just seemed outrageously out of order for life to throw a spanner in the works when things were getting better. Maybe that's selfish but that's how I felt. I wanted her to live, end of. Each night, when I went home to the flat by myself, I prayed, shouted, bribed and coerced, trying to convince God to let my mother live. There were times when I don't think I was very polite, being more desperate, terrified and angry.

My mum's operation was on Monday morning, and I sat in the hospital garden for the longest four hours of my life. At one stage a nurse came out to tell me that it wasn't going as expected and to prepare myself. I think the fact that I didn't have a father or any brothers and sisters to call at that point was a factor in me later wanting to have a big family.

After what seemed like a thousand years, I saw a gurney being carefully wheeled along the corridor. The hospital garden was right next to the ICU and I dashed inside, to see the hollowed face of my mother sticking out of the top of the white sheets. She wasn't awake but she was alive.

She stayed in ICU for over a week then graduated to a ward full of other cancer patients. At this time I started finding white feathers everywhere I went. I know this might sound strange, and as I've already said I was at the very start of spiritual understanding and had read no books about it at all at this stage, but I felt a wave of love and reassurance every time I found a feather. Now, before my accident, if anyone had tried to tell me that they were going through a hard time and kept finding feathers everywhere that seemed to be placed there especially for them, I would have probably tried to explain that they were from smelly old pigeons and suggested that the fanciful person didn't read too much into it. However! The pain I felt while my mum was in the ICU was so raw and real, I hated seeing her suffering, the feathers really did seem to turn up when I was feeling absolutely awful. I wasn't looking for them or expecting them, they were just there. And they really were everywhere, beautiful large white feathers, on stools, chairs, mostly on my bag and belongings or right in front of me, inside, outside, in places that feathers don't usually find their way to. And every time I found one, I felt a bit better. I felt loved, and I knew that everything would somehow be OK.

I recently searched online for this feather phenomenon and found many articles about it; this headline, "White feathers that convince Gloria Hunniford guardian angels do exist... and make her certain that her darling daughter Caron Keating is watching over her"[16] particularly caught my eye. Here is a quote from the article:

When she was alive, Caron – loved by millions for her TV and radio presenting roles – told me that an isolated white feather was an angel's calling card. And since her death, I am certain that she uses them to send messages to me. We were so close in life, and I am in no doubt that our bond has increased since her death. I am convinced that Caron – who died of breast cancer ten years ago, at the tragically young age of 41 – has been my guardian angel... The feathers started appearing – just when I most needed comfort, and leaving me in no doubt that Caron was indeed watching over me. The first time was in January 2005, nine months after her death. We were on our way to Disneyland Paris with her sons Charlie, ten, and Gabriel, seven. It was meant to be a birthday treat for Gabriel, but trudging along the rain-soaked platform at Folkestone, Kent, hand-in-hand with the boys, I felt consumed with memories. It wasn't just the lashing rain that dampened my mood. Every fibre ached with pain and despair as I thought of Caron... Then suddenly I looked down and there on my shoe was a single, snow-white feather. It had quite literally dropped from the sky. There was no rational explanation. Caron's words from long before she died came flooding back to me: "Remember, Mum. If an isolated white feather appears out of nowhere, it's a sign that your guardian angel is watching over you."... I know many people will brush aside the whole idea. I have to confess that I was once very sceptical too. Now... I am convinced she is always close to me, her pockets filled with feathers to drop at my feet when I need her comforting presence most.[17]

I have to say that although it probably wouldn't be a fact readily accepted by many people, I knew the feathers I was finding were put there to reassure and comfort me during a very difficult time, by angels or by God or by another amazing spiritual being. I never collected my feathers; I appreciated them and left them where they were. I would find them during difficult times until the end of my first year at university, when my mum was officially clear of any detectable cancer; thankfully she has been free of it ever since.

Chapter Five

Spiritual Journeying

From the moment I started university in September 1999, I had an enjoyable time creating my new life. This time round, my life had meaning, purpose and hope. Re-entering the world was terrifying and I had panic attacks in the early days as I tried to 'feel normal' and do 'normal things' like make new friends, go on nights out, write essays and enter into university life. Slowly, things became easier.

I became more confident talking about the accident, although I made light of it.

"Fell over while I was drunk," I'd smile. "Broke my arm and a few other bones." I had some impressive scars which I'd show, just for extra effect.

I was also becoming more confident about trying to explain how my consciousness had been alert and healthy during the first moments of the head injury. I tended to leave out the bit about leaving my body in case people thought it was weird. I'd read an article about how some people were found to be conscious during a coma, when they'd appeared completely unconscious. I can't find the exact article but here is an extract from a similar, later one:

Some patients who are in a coma may be aware of their surroundings even though they can't visibly communicate with others, and now, scientists have found a new way to help identify these patients. The researchers examined participants' brain waves using electroencephalography (EEG) and applied mathematical tools to the EEG data to find patterns of communication across brain regions. The researchers then compared these patterns in the comatose patients' brains with those of healthy people... Some comatose patients who were thought to be completely vegetative actually showed some patterns similar to those of healthy people.[18]

This discovery seemed to be the first concrete clue as to what had happened during those moments after the accident, but it didn't explain leaving my body.

By the time I graduated from the University of Reading in 2002 I was in what would become a three-year relationship with Pete. He was warm, loving, caring, funny and always emphasised that I should feel good about myself. Wonderful! We travelled to Australia, New Zealand and Fiji together that summer. I always had a feeling that we weren't meant to be together forever but it was a positive relationship while it lasted; we made a mutual decision to part company in the middle of 2003.

I met up with my father a few times between 2000 and 2003. I felt bolder now, and I wanted to hear some truths. I found myself saying what was on my mind more and more as the days went on – pre-accident I would have just kept any problems or worries to myself.

"You would have been glad if I'd died that day, wouldn't you?" I asked. "Your secret would have been erased forever."

"I don't want you to think that," he replied seriously. Hmm.

In 2003, I invited James round to my flat for a cup of tea. He declined, saying he didn't think it was appropriate. I'd been in a relationship with a man who valued me, Pete, who'd told me never to let anyone treat me badly. I was beginning to see that some men actually appreciated and respected me and thought me worth loving. I decided to stop seeing him and just write letters instead – doing this felt like I'd started to take a bit of control over my life. I only have one letter from him to me as I threw most of them away one day during a fit of feng shui, not wanting any objects with negative connotations in the house, and I never kept any copies of the letters I sent him.

In 2002, I had started my Master's degree at the Courtauld

Institute of Art, London, and graduated in the summer of 2003; then six months later, while training to be a teacher (I loved constantly studying but had come to the realisation that I needed to start paying back my humungous student debts) I met my future husband, Gareth, at a New Year's Eve party. I'd thrown myself into living life to the full at this point, and while I was aware that I hadn't fully come to terms with parts of the accident and even with the situation with my father, I put a block on those feelings, determined to forget about them and move on. My future husband turned out to be a tall, dark, handsome Welsh man. We didn't get together straight away, but when we did things happened quickly. Our first daughter was born in 2005 and our second in 2008; my growing family was the best thing to ever happen to me, it gave me a purpose, a home constantly full of love. Gareth is resolutely uninterested in religion and spirituality, although he listens to me talk incessantly about it with respect and patience. We are opposite in almost every way: he likes staying in, I like going out, he is cautious, I'm spontaneous, he likes things done in a sequence, I like to do things randomly, he likes to hoard money, I like to spend it, the list goes on. I feel he is the grounding force in our family; he keeps it real and is an amazing father. We married in 2011.

In 2007, while pregnant with my middle child, I started training to be a counsellor and psychotherapist at the WPF (Westminster Pastoral Foundation) in London. Since receiving effective therapy myself after being diagnosed with post-traumatic stress disorder I'd always wanted to train to be a counsellor with the hope that I could help others in a similar way. Part of the psychodynamic training was an 'experiential' group, which took place once a week. We all sat in a circle and basically shared anything, our lives, problems, grievances with each other; nothing was off limits. I got distinctions in all my essays during this time and I loved the training days, but I found the experiential group torture. I wasn't confident enough to keep speaking out in a large group of people I didn't know, let alone utter anything vaguely private about my life. Also, I didn't really understand my soul so how could I bare it in front of other people? And even if I wanted to, where would I start? I usually glossed over anything to do with my accident and father, fearing that too much intense information would make people run a mile. I people watched during these groups, absorbing who each person was, something I've always loved doing. Then one day I just blurted out everything to do with my father, who he was, how he hadn't wanted to meet me until I was fourteen, the accident, the whole shebang.

"Wow," said one of the other members of the group when I'd finished. "That was a long time coming but it was worth waiting for." Amazingly, everyone thought my father's actions were neglectful and abusive (for some reason I was half expecting them to defend him).

About a year after that I had a breakthrough moment: I suddenly understood that I'd be happier if I extracted myself from any hold he had over me; it was as though I'd come to terms with the fact that we'd never have a normal, loving father-daughter relationship, sad as that made me, and the best thing I could do was accept this, move completely away from it and get on with my life. I knew I'd be stronger away from it. James had made some gestures of care since the accident, sending me birthday presents and bits of money and I appreciated the effort taken; however, being in any sort of personal contact with him made me feel violated, although I can't explain exactly why. So I just stepped out of the game! And a twenty-ton weight lifted off my shoulders the moment I made the decision to stop trying, and accepted the situation for what it was.

In December 2007 my father wrote a letter to my mother:

Dear Emma,
Along with this letter I'm posting one for Hannah… As I say to her,
after a card and photo from Hannah last December, nothing else has
come…

Contact between them seemed to dry up after that and I have no more letters.

Raising my daughters and working part time as an art teacher kept me busy. I never stopped thinking about the day of the accident, constantly trying to make sense of it all, to get to the root of what had really happened, but there was still a gaping hole in my understanding. I'd heard the term 'near-death experience' bandied around and one day I decided to research it on the Internet. My search brought me to an account about Dr George Ritchie.

In 1943, at the age of 20, Dr. George G. Ritchie… was a private in the Army stationed in Texas awaiting a transfer to Richmond to study medicine at the Medical College of Virginia to become a doctor for the military. However, he got sick with pneumonia and died. The Army physician in charge stated in a notarized statement that the medical officer summoned detected "no evidence of respiration or cardiac impulse" and declared Ritchie dead. Ritchie had left his body in a near-death experience wandering around the hospital ward unaware he was dead. He found it strange no one could see him. He returned to his room and recognized his lifeless body, which had been covered with a sheet, by his fraternity ring. The room then became bright and Ritchie found himself in the presence of Jesus who then guided him through several realms of the afterlife before being told to return to his body. As the ward was preparing Ritchie's body for the morgue, he thought he detected movement in Ritchie's chest and called for a medical officer who provided a shot of adrenaline to the patient's heart causing him to breathe and his heart to beat. Ritchie then returned to life with one of the most important and profound NDEs ever documented.[19]

I found this fascinating but I didn't equate it with my experience, and talk of Jesus made me sceptical; I was becoming spiritual but not religious.

A few days later, unable to get Dr George Ritchie's compelling story out of my head, I typed "near death experience" into YouTube. Loads of different options appeared. The first video I clicked on was called *Life After Life* and I settled down to watch it with a cup of tea. Within minutes the tea was forgotten and I was leaning forwards towards the screen, absorbing every word. The documentary was about people who'd been very ill or injured and had left their body, some having very detailed spiritual journeys, which Dr Raymond Moody had coined "near-death experiences". I could relate to so much of what they said and how they felt. When the film finished I immediately searched for any books Dr Moody had written and bought them all, reading them in quick succession as soon as they arrived a few days later. I felt enlightened, dizzy with excitement. At last, somebody was explaining what had happened to me on the day of the accident, and what an explanation! It brought with it more questions than answers, but I was prepared to keep absorbing as much information about it as I could.

The first book I read by Dr Moody was *Life After Life*, closely followed by his *The Light Beyond*. He is

> most famous as an author of books about life after death and near-death experiences (NDE), a term that he coined in 1975 in his best-selling book *Life After Life*. Raymond Moody has spent around 44 years looking forward, trying to understand through his research what happens when people die. He is now recognized as the father of near-death experience psychology.[20]

Through his research, Dr Moody has broken down near-death experience elements into twelve parts, which are: a strange sound, peace and painlessness, out of body experience, the tunnel experience, rising rapidly into the heavens, people of light, the being of light, the life review, the reluctance to return, telling others

– most people realise that in our current society people will think them unstable if they mention their very real experience so generally elect to stay silent, effects on lives – generally broadened, deepened and transformed, and new views of death.[21] In his later book, *Reflections on Life After Life*, Dr Moody adds a few new elements: the vision of knowledge, cities of light, a realm of bewildered spirits and supernatural rescues. My NDE was relatively short so I didn't experience any of these new elements; Dannion Brinkley's book, *Secrets of the Light*, gives amazing first-hand accounts of crystal cities and a "fertile void" where these bewildered spirits roam.

When I first read about Dr Moody's original twelve elements, I could hardly believe my eyes, because I had experienced six of them: a strange sound, peace and painlessness, out of body experience, reluctance to return, a reluctance to tell others and a changed, transformed life. This was the biggest breakthrough in understanding the moments after the accident that I'd had yet. Lying there, listening to the ambulance arriving and then being taken to the first hospital, I had heard a strange grating sound and wondered what it was and when it would stop. I had felt amazingly peaceful, there had been no pain, just a feeling of being wrapped in love, and I had gone in and out of my body several times. And at the end, when the doctor had patted my hand vigorously while calling my name, I had felt reluctant to return to my body. I didn't feel I could tell anyone (apart from my mum) for ages in case they dismissed it or thought I was mad, and my life has definitely transformed since. I had to take some time to absorb the implications of what I now understood.

Following his years of research, Dr Moody's own beliefs are summed up in this quote from his interview with Jeffrey Mishlove:

> I don't mind saying that after talking with over a thousand people who have had these experiences, and having experienced many times some of the really baffling and unusual

features of these experiences, it has given me great confidence that there is a life after death. As a matter of fact, I must confess to you in all honesty, I have absolutely no doubt, on the basis of what my patients have told me, that they did get a glimpse of the beyond.[22]

I was blown away by understanding that I had experienced proof that there is life after death. I had still been alive while away from my body, and after reading the accounts in Dr Moody's books of many other near-death experiences, some far more in-depth than mine, I'd had my long-held suspicions confirmed: what I'd experienced that day hadn't just been dissociation like my therapist had suggested, I'd truly experienced life away from my body, I had experienced the reality of life going on after the body dies. It was true, very real and I now had an overwhelming desire to know as much as I possibly could about the subject. At the back of my mind I'd always known there was more to what had happened that day than I was comprehending, but I'd needed to physically and mentally heal first before I could properly comprehend the enormity of what had happened.

My first burning question was: what would have happened to me if I'd ignored the doctor's hand patting and carried on going up instead of going back down to my body? I read Dr Moody's books from cover to cover several times, absorbing other people's more in-depth and detailed experiences. Their accounts rang true to me and by allowing this belief to sink in a door opened in my mind and allowed an increasing amount of understanding to take place. In *The Light Beyond*, Dr Moody discusses a respected college professor's account of an NDE that took place during surgery:

I found myself floating up toward the ceiling, I could see everyone around the bed very plainly, even my own body. I thought how odd it was that they were upset about my body. I was fine and I wanted them to know that, but there seemed to be no way to let them know. It was as though there were a veil or a screen between me and the others in the room.

I became aware of an opening, if I can call it that. It appeared to be elongated and dark and I began to zoom through it. I was puzzled yet exhilarated. I came out of this tunnel into a realm of soft, brilliant love and light. The love was everywhere. It surrounded me and seemed to soak through into my very being. At some point I was shown, or saw, the events of my life. They were in a kind of vast panorama. All this is just really indescribable. People I knew who had died were there with me in the light, a friend who had died in college, my grandfather, and a great aunt, among others. They were happy, beaming.

I didn't want to go back, but I was told I had to by a man in light. I was being told I had not completed what I had to do in life. I came back into my body with a sudden lurch.[23]

Like me, Martha experienced the first three NDE elements but also the tunnel experience, people of light, a being of light, the life review and the reluctance to return. Because I'd experienced something similar to the beginning of her NDE I didn't have any trouble believing the rest of it, and it blew my mind. In fact all the accounts blew my mind because they opened up a whole new concept of life and death. There was no death, not in the way we traditionally thought of it; there was a change in states, from a physical one to a spiritual, but we were still us, we carried on existing. The implications of this seemed endless; the life review mentioned in so many accounts brought a new meaning to our life on earth. But before I looked any further into this I had to be very honest with myself: was there any chance that I was deluding myself here? After all, I had been in a very distressed state just before I fell, my thoughts had been whirling, disordered, troubled. And afterwards, during the time in the emergency room of the hospital I'd felt panic and stress. Could there be any chance that me leaving my body was just a distressed mind playing tricks on itself? I thought back to the interlude between the before and after of the accident, the time when I was actually popped back into my head then hovered around it; my thoughts and feelings at that time were *totally* different from just before the accident and after I opened my eyes. They were crystal clear, relaxed, calm, with a heightened awareness of what was going on. As I write this my mind is not distressed and disordered and I can tell the difference between when I've felt distressed and the calm, loving time when I knew who I was as I floated in and out of my head just after I fell. I have to honestly conclude that the experience actually happened and was not my distressed mind playing tricks on me. I also have to conclude that as I was suffering from severe head trauma at the time when my awareness and thoughts were at their most relaxed and clear: if consciousness was just inside the head I would never have experienced what I did; my consciousness would have been as bruised, broken and concussed as my actual head, not as it was – in top working order. In *The Light Beyond*, Dr Moody discusses other possible theories and explanations for NDEs such as carbon dioxide overload, birth as the tunnel experience, the NDE as hallucination and a comparison with schizophrenia. He concludes that none of the theories provides suitable evidence to explain an NDE.[24]

Dr Moody discussed many other cases in the same book, such as a businessman who, before his cardiac arrest, admitted he only had contempt for scholars, thinking they just researched and wrote without doing anything real:

But while the doctors were saying I was dead, this person I was with, this light... showed me a dimension of knowledge, I'll call it. I can't explain it anyway to you, but that's all right because every person on earth will see it for himself soon enough, whether they believe it now or not. Now that was a humbling experience for me. You can say I don't scorn professors anymore. Knowledge is important. I read everything I can get my hands on now, I really do... Some of it helps me understand my experience better... All of it does, in one way or another, because, as I say, when you have one of these experiences, you see that everything is connected.[25]

That is something people who've had in-depth NDEs frequently seem to report, that they see how everything is connected. I couldn't help wondering, as I read these incredible accounts, why my experience had just been a taster, a glimpse, compared to other more detailed NDEs. In a way I found myself wishing that it had been more in-depth, but then I was learning, via the wisdom of NDEs, that what happened to me and the length of my experience probably wasn't just a coincidence; it probably happened like that for a reason.

I took time to really think about and remember what happened on the day of the accident; I had hovered around my head, sometimes in it, sometimes away from it, going down through the trolley and then finally drawn upwards into the light. I, me, had been alive and kicking, on fantastic form in fact, *away* from my body. I could now accept this, although really I'd always known it was true. My head buzzed, I was walking on air for days; a whole new understanding was dawning in my mind. I felt like I'd found the Holy Grail and the meaning of life all in one go. I didn't talk to anyone about my discoveries at that stage; my husband saw the books I was reading lying around but didn't ask any questions, he was used to my 'quirky' tastes, the children were too young to take an interest, and I didn't broach the subject with anyone else. I knew that most people would think I was mad if I did and I could totally understand where they'd be coming from because I thought exactly like them until my accident. When Martha Todd told her parents about her NDE "they thought I had gone off the deep end" and her doctor told her parents that she was "delirious and halluci-nating".[26] I had a feeling I would receive similar reactions especially given the state I was in before the accident, so for the time being I concentrated on gaining as much personal under-standing as I could.

I ordered as many books about NDEs that I could find. Most accounts I read rang absolutely true, although very occasionally I would read one that felt fabricated or dramatized and that made me sad as it was a difficult enough subject to verify without people making things up. All the references I make in this book are to NDEs I feel are completely genuine.

One day, Anita Moorjani's book, *Dying To Be Me*, landed on my doormat. By then, I'd confided in one good friend who I thought would be interested in NDEs, and it turned out she already was. She recommended *Dying To Be Me* to me, saying it had changed her life. I read it as fast as I could and the result turned out to be another breakthrough; it felt like the most important one yet. I'm going to go into Anita Moorjani's story in detail because discovering it was such a pivotal moment in my life; it answered so many questions I'd had since the accident, but it also gave me much food for thought. Also, to explain how and where I've got to since the accident, it seems best to show the process that took me there. It might be worth mentioning that the title of this book is partly a nod to Anita and her work but also encapsulates how I feel about my experiences.

Anita Moorjani's medical records show that she was admitted to hospital on 2nd February 2006, about to end her battle with cancer – stage 4 lymphoma. She fell into a coma, but "knew when people came in to see me... The sharpness of my perception was even more intense than if I'd been awake and using my physical senses."[27] As she watched the nurses try and find her veins and the doctor stating she was drowning in her own fluid, Anita felt incredible:

> I felt no emotional attachment to my seemingly lifeless body as it lay there on the hospital bed... I felt free, liberated and magnificent... It was as though I'd been a prisoner in my own body for the past four years as the cancer ravaged my physical form, and at last I was being released.[28]

I could identify with Anita's experience so far; I remembered how sharp my own perception had felt after the fall. Because I trusted her account and had experienced something similar to the start of it, it felt natural to believe the rest, unbelievable as it may sound to some.

Anita felt herself being pulled away from the drama surrounding her body:

as though there were a bigger picture, a grander plan that was unfolding... I began to know that everything was perfect and going according to plan... I started to notice how I was continuing to expand to fill every space, until there was no separation between me and everything else... It was as though I were no longer restricted by the confines of space and time, and continued to spread myself out to occupy a greater expanse of consciousness.[29]

As I read Anita's account I found myself wondering whether I would have experienced the same thing had I chosen to go upwards not downwards and back into my body on the day of the accident. I half wished I'd experienced what she had.

Anita found herself wrapped in unconditional love: "love, joy, ecstasy and awe poured into me, through me and engulfed me. I was swallowed up and enveloped in more love than I ever knew existed."[30] Anita went on to meet her father, who'd died ten years earlier, and her best friend Soni, who'd died three years before. She says she saw her life:

intricately woven into everything I'd known so far. My experience was like a single thread woven through the huge and complexly colourful images of an infinite tapestry... Every single encounter was woven together to create the fabric that was the sum of my life up to this point. I may have been only one thread, yet I was integral to the overall finished picture.

Seeing this, I understood that I owed it to myself, to everyone I met, and to life itself to always be an expression of my own unique essence. Trying to be anything or anyone else didn't make me better – it just deprived me of my own true self! It kept others from experiencing me for who I am, and it deprived me of interacting authentically with them. Being inauthentic also deprives the universe of who I came here to be and what I came here to express.[31]

The content of this paragraph struck a massive chord with me. All my life I'd struggled to be who I really was. When you're a 'secret' and you're not supposed to exist as far as your father is concerned, it's hard to have the ability to be who you really are, to be confident in your own "unique essence". When one of your parents is essentially trying their hardest to cover up and deny your existence, developing your own identity and finding out who you really are becomes complex and confusing. I was presented with masses of irrefutable evidence of this a few years later, and will come back to it further on in the book. However, I'm not attributing all my low self-worth to the actions and choices of my father; in fact for several years I denied he'd had any impact on who I was at all. I began to see that it was how I chose to respond to his actions and choices that had the biggest impact on my life, and this became clear by reading the rest of *Dying To Be Me*.

During her NDE, Anita went on to question who she really was given the fact she continued to exist without her body, race, culture, religion or beliefs. I'd had the experience of separating from my body eight years before she did, in 1998, and had also wondered how on earth I continued to exist and be me away from my body. I felt very glad to have at last come across an account that might shed light on how and why.

There I was, without my body or any of my physical traits, yet my pure essence continued to exist, and it was *not* a reduced element of my whole self. In fact, it felt far greater and more intense and expansive than my physical being – magnificent in fact. I felt eternal, as if I'd always existed and always would without beginning or end. I was filled with the knowledge that I was simply magnificent!... *Just look at my life path! Why, oh why, have I always been so harsh with myself? Why was I always beating myself up? Why was I always forsaking myself? Why did I never stand up for myself and show the world the beauty of my own soul?... Why don't we realise this when we're in our physical bodies? How come I never knew that we're not supposed to be so tough on ourselves?*[32]

This could be me talking, and from reading other people's responses to Anita's book, these words could also have been spoken by thousands if not millions of people around the world. Without knowing I was doing it, I'd been so hard on myself about my father's attitude. I'd gone along with his need to keep me a secret and there had been many times when I'd said "yes" to him and various other people when I'd meant "no", because I was so afraid of more rejection. All the time, I had the choice to end that cycle, I just didn't know it. In saying this I do understand that of course other people can act in horrendous ways that are intended to hurt us, especially if they are emotionally, physically, psychologically and sexually abusive. But we all have the power to step out of their game whenever we want; we can't change what's happened to us or what the other person's done or continues to do, but we can choose how we feel about ourselves during every single moment of our lives. We can feel proud of ourselves, feel compassion and give ourselves a break. We can commend ourselves for our courage in the face of difficulty, for persevering, for choosing a different path. This can be extremely hard, especially in the face of someone else's abusive actions and does not mean we are condoning their actions or making light of what they've done. But the other person does not ultimately define who we are, we do. The other person will have to experience a life review, they will face what they've chosen to do then if not before. But it is not what they do to us but how we choose to feel about ourselves as a result of it that will affect us most profoundly. I kind of realised all this when I read *Dying To Be Me*.

One of the many interesting things about Anita Moorjani's case is that on 3rd February, thirty hours after she entered the coma, she opened her eyes, knowing that she was cured from stage 4 lymphoma, that all the tumours, lesions, toxic build-up and cancer cells would soon disappear. And they did. Two weeks after she'd been admitted, dying from advanced stage lymphoma, the radiologist couldn't find any in her body. He telephoned an oncologist. "I don't understand. I have scans that show this patient's lymphatic system was ridden with cancer two weeks ago, but now I can't find a lymph node on her body large enough to even suggest cancer."[33] Two separate oncologists, Dr Ko and Dr Long, became interested in Anita's story when they heard about it, and Dr Ko wrote up his own report after going through Anita's medical records. Here is an excerpt:

When I came to HKG (Hong Kong) last month, my intention was to scrutinize her clinical history, and to either validate or invalidate her claims. Having satisfied myself with the factual details, I actually find myself becoming more and more intrigued with her fantastic experience... especially the message she brought back... The morning of February 2 found her unable to get out of bed... The consensus was that she would not survive without intervention. While chemotherapy might be highly toxic in view of her multiple organ failure, it would be her only chance. During that night she underwent multiple examinations with MRI and CT, had 2 liters of fluid tapped from her chest, started on 3 of 7 chemotherapy drugs, and was placed in the ICU. This was when Anita drifted off into what she described as her NDE... The evening of Feb 3, Anita awoke, sat up, and declared to her family she would be okay... Based on my own experience and opinions of several colleagues, I am unable to attribute her dramatic recovery to her chemotherapy. Based on what we have learned about cancer cell behaviours, I speculate that something (non-physical 'information'?) either switched off the mutated genes from expressing, or signaled them to a programed cell death. The exact mechanism is unknown to us, but not likely to be the result of cytotoxic drugs. I think my encounter with Anita's experience shall set the stage for me to learn more about this phenomenon, and about the true nature of ourselves![34]

Anita says that during her NDE, she:

became aware that we're all connected... the interwoven unification felt as though it were expanding outward to include everything in the universe – every human, animal, plant, insect, mountain, sea, inanimate object and the cosmos. I realised that the entire universe is alive and infused with consciousness, encompassing all of life and nature. Everything belongs to an infinite Whole. I was intricately, inseparably enmeshed with all of life. We're all facets of that unity – we're *all* One, and each of us has an effect on the collective Whole... I also understood that the cancer was not some punishment for anything I'd done wrong, nor was I experiencing negative karma as a result of any of my actions, as I'd previously believed. It was as though every moment held infinite possibilities, and where I was at that point in time was a culmination of every decision, every choice, and every thought of my entire life. My many fears and my great power had manifested as this disease.[35]

Now, as I found that Anita's words greatly expanded on my own NDE, I applied her understanding of how her cancer came about to my own life. Up until just after the accident, I'd been full of fears for years: fears of rejection, abandonment, that I wasn't good enough, that I wasn't lovable, the list goes on. Perhaps, if I'd gone up instead of down that day during the NDE, I would have seen how my own repressed power had manifested itself in pain in my mind. Since the accident I was growing stronger and happier, but was very aware that many jigsaw pieces in the puzzle of my life were still missing. Anita Moorjani's book helped to find some of those pieces and slot them into place. It may not have been solely my response to my father's actions (i.e. internalising pain) that led me to becoming so run-down and unable to look after myself that the accident occurred; maybe I'd internalised other pain and stresses too, but I do think it was a major factor. It has been suggested that we choose our lives before we even come here, so perhaps I chose all this. Although I could have responded to each decision in my life differently and therefore have created a different history, dealing with my father's choices was clearly always going to be a challenge.

Since her recovery, Anita's life has transformed. She travels the world talking about her experience, and her most important message to everyone is to "realise your own magnificence and to express yourself fearlessly in the world."[36] She says, "The only universal solution I have is to love yourself unconditionally and be yourself fearlessly! This is the most important lesson I learned from my NDE."[37] These are wise words indeed; however, when I first read them they pinpointed one of the main problems in my life: I didn't love myself unconditionally and I wasn't being myself fearlessly. I was getting quite good at acting as though I was OK, but really I couldn't forgive myself for causing the accident in the first place.

Life was starting to make more sense. Not just my life on earth, but life in its entirety. I was now ready to talk more about my experience, having been given the vocabulary to explain it through NDE research, but I didn't know who to. In fact I was starting to have a burning desire to talk about it. I researched "near-death experiences UK" on the Internet and eventually found Dr Penny

Sartori's contact details – she seemed to be one of the only people in the UK researching NDEs. I emailed her, asking if she knew of any people who'd had NDEs who met up with each other as I'd seen on the Internet that in the United States it was common for NDE survivors to meet for support and to share experiences. I also explained what had happened to me and queried the counsellor's diagnosis of dissociation. Interestingly Dr Penny Sartori has not had an NDE herself but has become convinced of their existence through working in intensive care units looking after dying patients; an experience she discusses in depth in her book, *The Wisdom of Near-Death Experiences*. In January 2014, she sent this reply:

Dear Hannah,

Your experience is fascinating to me and I am also interested by the amazing life changes after your experience and your healing after such serious injuries. What you have described is consistent with many other people's experiences. I've been studying these for 20 years now and they are extremely important experiences that science is now taking notice of (although there are still many sceptics out there too).

Your counsellor is quite correct, dissociation is a response to stress and people usually find themselves looking down on the situation from above. What you experienced is an out of body experience which is one of the components of a near-death experience (NDE). So what you experienced was some dissociation but NDEs are far more than just dissociation. NDEs are a very complex phenomenon and at present there are no theories that adequately explain them. There have been many scientific investigations to see if they are due to lack of oxygen or the drugs administered at the time of the emergency but these are not sufficient explanations.

What these experiences appear to be showing is that the current scientific explanation that consciousness is a by-product of the brain is not correct. It seems that a heightened state of consciousness is primary and exists around us all the time but we are not aware of it because the brain screens it out. However, there are times when the brain can become dysfunctional (as yours did due to traumatic injury) and is no longer able to screen out this consciousness. Consequently the person will experience consciousness in its purest form that is not usually perceived when in the normal state of consciousness. That is why you didn't register that you were unconscious and described feeling great clarity etc. There is so much more to say on this subject but I'm not sure if I'm bombarding you with too much information. I've written a book about NDEs called The Wisdom of Near-Death Experiences *which looks at various different aspects of them as well as possible explanations and includes many examples from people I have met or written to. It will be out on 18*th *February.*

I'm hoping to arrange a meeting at some point later in the year with the other 2 ladies who are interested in setting up a support group so people who have had NDEs can meet each other and chat about their experiences. As soon as I make any progress I'll be in touch as it would be great to meet up with you at some point and discuss your experience in more depth.

Thank you so much for sharing your experience. Would you mind if I keep it in my files and possibly use it for a future publication? I won't mention your name (unless you are happy for me to do so).

Best wishes

Penny

This email was wonderful to read because it validated my own assessment of what had happened: "What you experienced is an out of body experience which is one of the components of a near-death experience (NDE)." I felt very heartened by the fact that medical staff like Dr Sartori, through their own observations and experiences, are now seriously studying the NDE phenomenon. In *The Wisdom of Near-Death Experiences,* Dr Sartori writes:

once I read about NDEs there was no turning back as I was compelled to learn more. My original scepticism – which I once believed to be rational – I now view as irrational, because at the time I was judging NDEs from a pre-conceived perspective and did not have an open mind to other possibilities and no in-depth knowledge of them. It is only since I was forced to look at the wider picture and think outside the box by fully engaging with the range of complexities associated with NDEs that I realized my previous explanations were wrong and miscon-ceived.[38]

Like Dr Sartori, I'd realised that my previous perceptions (pre-accident) of what happened when you died were mistaken. I had first-hand experience that life went on away from your body and I wasn't going to waste that insight. I now wanted to understand what near-death experiences were telling us, to find out what the implications were regarding life after death and our life here on earth. It seemed there was so much we could learn from everyone's NDEs if we really looked at them.

While I continued to avidly research NDEs, I was surprised to find myself increasingly consumed by rage. This may have also been to do with the fact that I was watching my husband parent our children, and how naturally paternal love came to him, and how they responded. This was everything I'd wanted for my children so I was ecstatic on this count. However, I was becoming mightily furious that my father had denied me the chance of growing up knowing his family, his sisters, parents, nephews and brothers-in-law. I knew his parents had died without knowing they had a granddaughter and my father always flatly refused to consider telling his sisters and other relatives about me; his attitude seemed to contradict everything that I was learning from my own experience and from other NDEs.

All I knew about my mysterious relatives were their names – my father must have told my mother about them during their relationship. Overtaken by a strong desire to know that side of the family, I decided to search for clues as to my aunt and uncle,

Marion and Richard Webster, on the Internet (my father's sister and her husband). I found Richard's work email address. Here is an extract from the email my husband sent to Richard in January 2011 on my behalf:

Dear Richard,

I am writing to you on behalf of my wife, Hannah. I realise this may be an unusual email to receive but Hannah and I would be very grateful if you could share the contents of it with your wife, Marion. Hannah is the daughter of Marion's brother, James Carson... Hannah has known your names for some time... (and) recently found your email address... and she would very much like to meet her Aunt, Marion. James has made it clear over the years that he is unable or unwilling to have a father/daughter relationship with Hannah. Unfortunately, James has also put considerable pressure on Hannah over the years to keep her existence secret from his family. I'm sorry to say that his superiors in the Catholic Church have reinforced this message, both to Hannah and her mother, much preferring that the daughter of a Catholic priest keep silent about her parentage. No doubt you can imagine the impact such pressure has on an individual, and this is the main reason why Hannah has not attempted to contact her family until now. Hannah would like to give... (her aunts) the opportunity to get in touch with her as she would dearly love to know about the Carson side of the family... Hannah is aware that she has two aunts and four cousins that may know nothing of her existence, and would like to give them the opportunity to get in touch. She means James no ill will, but would just like to create a positive opening for contact with her aunts... If Marion would like to meet her niece please could you email me back and I will pass your emails to Hannah.

Best wishes,
Gareth

Three days later, Richard replied. This was the moment I'd imagined for many years, and could hardly believe it was happening:

Dear Gareth,

Marion died in November 2007... I don't believe Marion knew anything about this story, and I have been trying to get a copy of Hannah's birth certificate, but I don't know the exact date of birth... Needless to say, I was interested to get more information before I broached the subject with James (I did not know the details you mention in your email and the reprehensible behaviour of the church authorities). I'm sure Marion would agree with me that this sort of secrecy is beyond the pale, and she would be keen to meet you all. Here is a niece and her family who are unable to communicate with paternal relatives. I am surprised he did not even enlighten his mother... So personally I would be very happy to meet your family... Thank you for these 2 momentous communications,

Richard

I was very sad to hear that Marion had died, but I was ecstatic that channels of communication with my unknown side of the family were now open. I started emailing Richard directly and we arranged that he would come over to our house for lunch that Sunday. I then received this email from him:

Dear Hannah,

Have been in touch with James by email and had reply, he is not keen on my visiting (you) but I am not convinced this should be a problem. He invited me to visit him (doesn't know I have a visit planned) on Saturday which I accepted.

Looking forward to seeing you Sunday,
Best wishes,
Richard

As soon as I heard that Richard was meeting James the day before he visited us, I had a bad feeling; I just knew things were about to go rather wrong. When Richard came to visit his enthusiasm to meet us had been replaced with nervous suspicion. The day before, my father had tried to convince him not to come and see me, but Richard had decided to anyway. James had shown him a list of payments he'd made to my mother and I, and persuaded Richard that he'd done his best as a father. He also suggested that it would not be appropriate for my other aunt, who is still alive, to learn of my existence due to her alleged mental problems, and that he'd prefer Richard's sons, my cousins, not to get to know me. Richard seemed to agree with him on many counts, having known James for the majority of his life and not knowing me at all, although he did say that he'd spoken at James' ordination at James' request, and wished he'd known James had a child at that point as his decision to make a speech might have been different. Contact between him and I soon stopped. I met his sons a few times; they had been spoken to by James too, he'd urged them not to get to know me, not to tell their children that we were related, so effectively the link would die out anyway. They were kind, but I had a feeling they viewed me with suspicion, and asked me more than once what my "next move" was, as though I had an elaborate plan. I just wanted to be accepted by that side of the family, but had to admit defeat. This whole episode made me feel sad.

I now appreciated my amazing mother, husband, children, friends and family (on my mother's side) even more (if that was possible). I knew I was lucky to be surrounded by people who loved me and it was important to keep things in perspective. I'd already lived through the dark consequences of internalising that kind of pain before – and I now knew I could choose not to let it make me feel bad. Luckily, the knowledge and wisdom I continued to absorb from NDE research was just the boost I needed to achieve this.

I noticed that many accounts about NDEs recorded that survivors felt they'd been "allowed" to live because they'd not yet fulfilled their "purpose". In *Reflections on Life After Life* Dr Moody writes that after an NDE people often "relate that afterward their lives were changed... they came to feel they were saved from death for a purpose."[39] Dannion Brinkley, who, during his NDE, had understood he must build meditation centres, became obsessed with this purpose. "Sandy and I finally divorced when the constant talk about the experience and the need to build the centres became too much for her. I couldn't blame her. Near-death experiences are hard on couples."[40] Since the accident I'd turned the question of why I'd survived over and over in my head; I was relieved that I had but also knew that people had been killed by shorter falls or more minor accidents. I'd always felt that it was because I had more to do in this life but was having trouble pinpointing exactly what it was that I was supposed to be doing. Was it being a daughter, mother, wife and friend? If so I was fulfilling those roles and enjoying them enormously but felt there was more I needed to do.

By 2012, I was the happiest I could remember being. On one level I knew there were aspects of my previous life that I hadn't come to terms with, but things seemed to be ticking along quite nicely with me squashing these aspects down and pretending they didn't exist – I presumed that that's what all adults did – it seemed like an excellent and effective coping strategy. The crazy, raw energy I'd felt after healing was now calmer, thanks to meditation, and I could channel it more effectively where I needed to. My son was born at the end of 2012, then in 2013, while on maternity leave from my teaching job, I had an urge to write a children's book for my daughters. They were enthusiastic about it (I knew they'd be honest – they'd quite rightly identified a previous story as mind-blowingly dull), so I published it myself on CreateSpace then sent it to several publishers. Amazingly it has now been published under a pen name by independent publishers and has sold over 10,000 copies in three years. Having my name, albeit a kind of pseudonym, appearing on the Internet in a modest kind of way felt like a step away from the confines of secrecy. It was scary but excellent.

On 28th February 2015, I went to Hay House's one-day workshop "Being Myself", run by Anita Moorjani. My good friend, who'd recommended Anita's book to me, came too. We were both slightly nervous in case Anita came across as in some way false or disingenuous; we'd both found her book *Dying To Be Me* so life changing and inspiring and didn't want to be disillusioned but were prepared to be honest with each other about our gut feelings. But we needn't have worried; Anita was warm and genuine, and I felt she was being completely truthful about her experience. Quite early on in the day I noticed that there was a shining, pale gold border outlining Anita that followed her about wherever she went. It was particularly bright and precise around her head. I looked up at the ceiling in case she had special lighting on her – she was standing on a platform in the centre of a large hall. But there were no spotlights on her, just a huge skylight above her. I didn't mention this shining border to my friend, just watched it continuously throughout the day, wondering if I was seeing Anita's aura. I'd never seen one before, and looked it up on the Internet when I got home; what I'd seen did seem to correlate with aura descriptions. Quite excited about this discovery, I mentioned it to my husband, whose instant reaction was to announce that I was barking mad. I've since found I can see other people's auras, although I know that will sound unbelievable, especially to my husband!

Dr David Hamilton was also speaking at the Hay House event. I'd never heard of him before but was interested in what he had to say about his new book, *I Heart Me*, because it tackled the awkward issues surrounding the problem of how to truly love ourselves. As my own effort at that was a struggling work in progress that wasn't really getting anywhere, I decided to buy his book. I needed help breaking through an invisible barrier that seemed to be made from a mixture of low self-worth at being a 'secret', Catholic guilt, guilt and shame at causing the accident and generally being too British to accept that loving myself was OK. It felt like the layers I had to drill through to get anywhere near the core were endless and made from concrete. Intellectually I knew I should feel good about myself – it seems a sensible psychological angle to adopt for good mental health – and there were many things I *did* feel good about, namely my children, husband, family, friends, books and teaching job, but equally I knew there was no point pretending I felt great about *me* when I actually didn't and couldn't. I enjoyed Dr Hamilton's book so much that I bought another by him, *It's The Thought That Counts: Why Mind Over Matter Really Works*.

In it, Dr Hamilton says, "Everything that exists was born in the quantum field" and that this theory parallels that of Eastern Mystical teaching, with the only difference being that "what we call 'the quantum field' they call 'a field of *qi*' or 'a field of conscious intelligence'... If you take the Eastern belief, then at the most basic level everything is composed of consciousness."[41] I was intrigued by his words; if Dr Hamilton had drawn a parallel between consciousness and the quantum field, I wondered if anyone else had. I discovered that indeed they had while reading Pim van Lommel's book, *Consciousness Beyond Life: The Science of the Near-Death Experience*, in which the author argues that:

> some prospective and many retrospective studies of near-death experiences have shown that various aspects of an NDE correspond with or are analogous to some of the basic principles from quantum theory, such as nonlocality, entanglement or interconnectedness, and instantaneous information exchange in a timeless and placeless dimension. I believe that while quantum physics cannot explain the origins of our consciousness, nonlocal consciousness does have a lot of common ground with widely accepted concepts from quantum theory. So in my opinion, quantum physics could also help us understand the transition from consciousness in nonlocal space to our physical brain.[42]

I wonder how many other people have drawn a connection between quantum theory and near-death experiences. This connection could provide an opening for people more interested in science than spirituality to become involved with the phenomenon of NDEs. I do believe that science and spirituality are not actually separate from each other at all, as they can sometimes seem; they are both slices of the same cake, fingers belonging to the same hand. Research into each provides different discourses and understanding about the same subject: our universe and how and why we are in it. As Einstein said, "All religions, arts and sciences are branches of the same tree." Carl Sagan said, "The fervently hoped notion that science and spirituality are somehow mutually exclusive does a disservice to both."[43] Perhaps near-death experiences bridge the gap, however fleetingly, between the two.

In March 2015, my husband and I took a leap of faith and moved our family into the depths of the countryside, something we'd been thinking of doing for quite some time. In the weeks leading up to the move I was so excited, thinking about the beautiful views we'd be surrounded by, the quieter pace of life, the leafy garden for the children. I feel at my calmest while surrounded by nature, and at my most stressed in a city. But a week or so after we moved in, I had an emotional crash. The familiar sadness, always in the background somewhere, was back. This annoyed me intensely, I wanted to enjoy my new life, not always be fighting off sadness – so I decided to get to the bottom of it once and for all, even if it meant delving into areas such as my relationship with my father and the accident which I'd already successfully cordoned off.

As soon as I made the decision to get to the bottom of the sadness, things happened fast. The next day I mentioned to my mum that I might like to see a therapist for a few weeks to sort some stuff out and she said that was funny, her friend had just been singing the praises of a therapist named Elizabeth, who'd really helped someone close to her. Soon, I had Elizabeth's number, and a meeting was arranged. I was a bit nervous before I arrived, wondering if I'd made the right decision to come, but when I met Elizabeth for the first time I knew I had. We started to talk, then something unexpected happened. I explained, tentatively, about the accident and that I'd left my body through my head. I usually gloss over this bit, since most people assume it was just a by-product of being so close to death, but Elizabeth was interested. I mentioned that I thought it was a near-death experience and she agreed! She understood!

"I wouldn't say this normally in counselling sessions, but I can tell you've had a spiritual experience," she said, getting up to take a book down from a shelf above me. "Why don't you read this?"

It was a book by Don Piper called *90 Minutes in Heaven: A True Story of Death and Life.*

"Wow," I said, feeling gobsmacked and flabbergasted.

It was clear that as well as being an excellent and experienced therapist, Elizabeth was also very spiritual, and was particularly interested in angels. I began to wonder if she was an angel herself at one stage; I couldn't believe I'd met someone who would understand literally all parts of my life and be able to help me shed light on them. Usually counsellors (that I'd met so far) concentrated on a theoretical model but didn't address spirituality. Now I felt like a door had opened and I was in an absolute rush to run through it.

Through talking to Elizabeth I began to see a relationship between my NDE and my father's actions. At that point I understood how my father's actions and my NDE were connected; I'd felt they were linked for some time and now that I could see how, my whole life started to make sense.

My NDE showed me what real love – all-encompassing, accepting, unconditional love – is, and that I'm worthy of it. It stepped in when I'd reached the bottom of a destructive spiral culminating in the accident and surrounded me with a loving acceptance, compassion and peace, drawing me up into the light as a taster before making it clear I had to go back and open my eyes. It showed me who I really was, what it felt like not to feel fear or to feel worthless. Basically, it was a massive wake-up call. It showed me that contrary to what I'd felt previously, I was loved and valued, and this knowledge became the biggest and most important jigsaw piece that I needed to put my life together. I came back to continue the journey, finding more jigsaw pieces along the way. My father, a 'man of God', rejected me, whereas the love and light during the NDE accepted me; showing that decisions to reject a child on earth in the name of God (by any name) are false and unfounded, the real God loves me (and everyone else) unconditionally.

The point about God loving all children of priests (and everyone else) unconditionally is an important one because it challenges so many decisions made by the Catholic Church that are still upheld. It was as though the love and light were making that point intentionally; when priests reject their children and treat them without love in the name of God, they don't speak for God, who continues to love those children and I suspect would rather like those priests to do the same. By nearly dying and having a glimpse of the love and acceptance on the 'other side', then returning to health, I was given the opportunity to learn how to love and be proud to be myself and to understand my value; I don't know why, exactly, but I was, and I'm very grateful for that chance. I think that's why I still felt a background sadness, because I was still letting the secrecy have a hold over me; I'd given the power of fully being myself over to fear. I can only hope that my story helps to end the veil of silence covering priests' children all over the world. It's time to end it now, there is no reason why priests can't be good fathers and good priests; Anglican priests have been doing it for years.

I have no wish to say anything against religion that will offend people – I have some good friends and family who are devoutly religious and the nuns who worked at my school were amazing. Clearly, many good people deeply believe in one religion or another, and it works for them. My own view is more spiritual; I believe we are all part of the same experience. I only have a problem with religion when negative or destructive actions are executed in the name of God. If God is love then these negative or destructive actions are working against love not for love, and are therefore hypocritical. Kenneth Ring, a psychology professor from Connecticut, discovered through his research that NDEs can happen to anyone that holds any type of religious belief, or indeed no religious belief, including atheists. NDEs are inclusive! The study Ring "devised examined the stories of 102 near-death experiencers and showed that religion is no more a factor in a person having an NDE than age or race. In short, he proved that near-death experiences are equal opportunity events."[44] Anita Moorjani, brought up in the Hindu tradition, felt that:

> During my NDE, I discovered that in listening to all these external voices (e.g. religious teachings) I'd lost myself... So these days, I don't follow any established methodology, order, ritual, dogma, or doctrine. In fact, one of my biggest rules is that there should never be any hard and fast rules!... I'm not saying I'm against organised religion, but I am sceptical of any message when it leads to all the divisiveness, strife and killing that go on in this world in the name of religion, when in truth, we're all One – all facets of the same Whole. Human beings are so varied that some fare better with organised religion or spiritual paths, whereas others don't... To advocate any option or doctrine as being the one true way would only serve to limit who we are and what we've come here to be.[45]

I think part of the reason I went through this, discovering my identity amid the secrecy of the Catholic Church and an NDE, was to discover that if I'd followed the advice of the Church forever, I would essentially be annihilating the real me. I'd be in cahoots with the notion that priests' children shouldn't be known to exist, so I've had to cut through this to find my own identity. Catholic clericalism and doctrine isn't always right; I now know how important it is to never lose my own truth among someone else's rules. What appears to be true because religious figures say it is sometimes just isn't. As I now realise, it's not easy to stand up for what you believe in, especially when there is a weighty institution indoctrinating priests, mothers and children in the need for confidentiality. But as the facts show, this secrecy is not really good for anyone in the long run, especially if it annihilates the child's sense of identity.

Another breakthrough came a few days after I met Elizabeth for the first time. I decided to do an Internet search about children fathered by Catholic priests; if I was going to get to the bottom of the confusing feelings I felt about this I wanted to be as well informed as possible. I was expecting a few newspaper articles so was astounded to come across a site called "Coping International". I immediately clicked on it and had a spine-tingling moment as I read about what Coping International stands for and does. I could hardly believe what I was seeing – here was a site solely dedicated to supporting the children of priests. My first thought was, "Hurray! I'm not the only one!" I felt insanely happy to have found a bunch of people in a similar situation to myself; never before had I met anyone whose father was a Catholic priest.

I read on, amazed to discover that Coping International is endorsed by some very high profile figures including the Pope. Part of a letter to Coping International on behalf of Pope Francis, dated 2014, reads, "Please be assured of His Holiness' appreciation for the Concerns and charitable sentiments that motivate your initiatives together with a remembrance in his prayers." Wow! Why hadn't I heard of Coping International before? "The state of pure allowing seems like the place where most positive change can occur. Let yourself be you, no matter who you are, embracing anything that makes you feel alive."[46] Maybe I was just ready to allow changes to take place, whereas I hadn't been ready before. Archbishop Diarmuid Martin said, "I pray that Coping will be able to find ways which will bring the children of priests and their natural parents together for the benefit of both." An excerpt of a letter from the Irish Catholic Bishops to Coping reads:

The Irish Catholic Bishops recognise the significance and importance of adequate care being provided for children born to priests [...] and are anxious to ensure that appropriate support is being offered to all children. In particular they appreciate the sensitivity required in any pastoral outreach to children of priests. The bishops are actively collaborating with Towards Healing so that Towards Healing will be in a position to provide appropriate counselling/support to children of Catholic clergy. [...] Confidentiality agreements may be unjust if they hinder the basic goods of the mother and child, example: if they are used to protect the reputation of the priest or institutional church by creating a veil of secrecy that isolates the mother and child, from relationships, knowledge and resources, which they are owed in natural justice.

Mairead McGuiness, Vice President of the European Parliament and Children's Rights Mediator, said:

The organisation (Coping) will provide a forum for those impacted to speak about their experiences in a compassionate and professional environment. By recognising the work of Coping International, individuals who previously had no formal support structure will now have a forum in which to share their experiences, thus helping to destigmatise this issue.

Wow, in fact, wow times infinity. I suddenly felt strong, like I could climb the tallest mountain in the world without stopping for a break. I wasn't alone in this weird situation. And there was help out there! Unbelievable; it was truly a great day when I discovered Coping International. I quickly sent them an email, unsure who was running it and if I'd ever receive one back. But later that day I did, from the amazing coordinator of Coping, that started, "How wonderful to hear from you," and I can honestly say that I felt some deep healing begin at that moment.

Since then, I've been in regular contact with Coping and my testimony is now on their website, alongside several others. I have by no means experienced the worst rejection. Jack Finnegan's (some names on the site are pseudonyms) reads:

> Since I was a young lad I can never remember having a strong sense of who I was... and lived my life in a fearful state at the whims of the world and others. This fear which I ingested had its hallmarks from my youth and I could never explain its presence in my life... after suffering for years with mental ill-health and seeking answers and causes to my struggles, I eventually found out the truth, that the man I was conceived by was a Catholic priest... I commenced a very painful journey to meet this man, my father, and to get to know him. I wanted to understand why he made the decisions he did in his life and in doing so to perhaps heal the hurt that lay within me.

I was struck by the similarities between Jack's story and my own, and I didn't think it was a coincidence that we'd had similar difficulties to deal with. Lloyd Johnson's testimony reads:

> I was born in the mid-eighties and grew up with a particular syndrome that was both untraceable and undefinable, yet it had very particular characteristics. It made me suffer endlessly. Psychological trauma is a terrible thing to endure as it bears no physical mark and thus people do not believe that you are actually suffering at all and just mark you as 'odd', 'different'... I grew close to the parish priest from a very young age and we had an enduring and endearing relationship. I served mass and spent time with him as he became a family friend... When he died in my late teenage years, I became intensely isolated following his untimely death. I withdrew into myself and could not fathom why this man's death would have such an effect upon me?... But then a Saturday night arrived many, many years

following his death... "He is my real father, isn't he?" I voiced the words to my mother... my whole self, clicked. It was as if two Lego pieces came together suddenly and without expectancy.

Again, I felt a connection to Lloyd through his story; I could identify with it, although in some ways his experience was different from my own. Patricia Bond's son, Nathan, was baptized by his own father, then "waited his entire life to know this man... he suffered alone often asking me why his father chose wine over blood, referring to his father's choice of remaining in the priesthood and giving up his own son. Nathan never knew how to express his feelings until it was too late", he was diagnosed with a brain tumour aged nineteen and died in 2009. "Nathan's dying wish was to help others like him and through the wondrous works of Coping International my son will see his wish come true. Others like him (children born to Catholic Priests) will find the professional guidance should they need through counselling, with the support and not the denial of our Holy Catholic Church." There are many more testimonies on the site that describe trust issues, emotional abandonment and a priest who organised his own daughter's adoption, among other matters. I find Simon Bello's account the most harrowing:

I am the son of a priest, a Catholic Missionary who worked in Africa his entire life. I was the product of a rape by this man. The parish priest at the time concealed the identity of my natural father and without concern for either mother or child, left the child minus dignity, asking very natural questions of a young single mother in 1952 in Uganda... The Catholic Church in 1952 would go on to conceal the rape. The identity of her abuser, the father of her child would receive no action against him.

This is shocking on every level.

What is the common denominator here, that ties all our testimonies together, and affects us – despite our differing experiences – in the same way? I think Coping International has hit the nail on the head when they say, "To be buried beneath a secret can have devastating effects." It's the *secrecy* that bonds each case together, and that is ultimately so destructive. Coping have looked into the mental health issues surrounding children of priests and say that "mental health lies at the core of what Coping International stands for, what Coping is all about." They cite "genealogical bewilderment" – a term coined by HJ Sants – as the main problem.

> [A] genealogically bewildered child is one who has no knowledge of his [or her] natural parents or only uncertain knowledge of them [thus] undermining his [or her] security and mental health… It may create a sense of ontological insecurity or anxiousness… Children with unknown parents may not always show overt concern about their lack at every stage of development, but clinical knowledge of such children suggests that at some time, very often in early adolescence, they will begin searching for clues.[47]

Coping also states that, "Secrecy can be an enormous burden to carry. It may weigh upon the interior relationship between the mother and her child for the duration of both of their lifetimes affecting both, whether consciously or unconsciously."[48] Well, that explains a lot.

I explained my whole situation to Coping International, including the meeting in 1977 between my mother, father and Frank Harding, where the secrecy plan was hatched. Frank's later letter implies that my mother was complicit with the plan but her own letter clearly states that her one request, that no decision was made until after the baby was born, was ignored and overridden. Coping said the priests made a verbal confidentiality agreement with my mother rather than a written one, and that recently the Irish Catholics Bishops Conference states that:

> Confidentiality agreements may be unjust if they hinder the basic goods of the mother and child, example: if they are used to protect the reputation of the priest or institutional church by creating a veil of secrecy that isolates the mother and child, from relationships, knowledge and resources, which they are owed in natural justice.[49]

In my case the verbal confidentiality agreement was undeniably made to protect the reputation of my father.

The coordinator of Coping sent me a draft letter in July 2015, which he asked if I'd like him to send to a senior church official in the UK, the United Nations Children's Rights Commissioner (as part of the letter is for UPR UN) and the Vatican, as Pope Francis is kept abreast of everything Coping does. He explained that Coping, which is about openness while simultaneously protecting clients, wants to open up the truth about this secrecy. This is an excerpt from the draft letter:

> *I write to you with the good expectation that you will consider what it is I have to say regarding... a client of Coping. Please understand that Coping wishes only for a child centred response to a situation that is of grave concern for both us and undoubtedly you too... Most recently Coping has been contacted by lady... Communication has been frequent between Coping and Hannah for some time now and overall in my capacity as coordinator of Coping and as a counsellor; I would have grave concerns for Hannah, given the conduct of some hierarchical members of your diocese, unfortunately including a late Cardinal. She has expressed that at least one priest, as well as the late Cardinal by means of letters, initiated and participated in efforts that were intended to suppress Hannah's knowledge and a full reciprocal, loving relationship with her natural father. James Carson too, it would*

seem, went along with, or at the very least, acted in a manner that was akin to the underhand tactics of the diocese for a period that has spanned Hannah's natural life to this date.

Sadly, she still feels as if she is in a difficult place that is because, she is. Her love for her natural father has been placed in opposition to her very natural desire to lead a normal, open life, whereupon no secrecy is imposed upon her, nor intended toward her. This is conducive toward emotional abuse and direct neglect not only on behalf of James Carson, but the diocese too… What does one do for, or how does one respond to a lady who was ignored and mistreated and her daughter for so long, so deliberately…? To begin with, an apology from you on behalf of the diocese in person to both Hannah and her mother would be a good place to start. An apology that acknowledges the true nature of the Catholic Church, a structure that of itself ought to simmer as a reflective light, the familial unit, certainly not as an instrument of refraction… I urge a word of caution to anyone who in anyway perpetuates a grievance that may be understood as an attempt to dissuade Hannah from truth, her own life of happiness or honesty and forthrightness. This certainly would not be in tune with a considered Catholic ethos nor would it be either person centred or child centred as an act, certainly not priestly.

My immediate thought was "Yes, let's do this!" Having someone acting on my behalf against the powerful institution that is the Catholic Church felt like a breath of fresh air. I felt stronger and empowered just reading the draft letter. But I buckled the next day, suddenly feeling awful. I think it was fear; I'd been suppressed, receiving polite threats for so many years that the idea of speaking out was suddenly terrifying. So, feeling like a coward, I told Coping I needed more time to think about sending the letter. I knew I wanted to help uncover the secrecy about priests' children, but doing something against my father made me feel physically sick, not because I wanted to protect him but because he'd convinced me that terrible things would happen if I did. I expressed my fears to

Coping who said they believed that keeping a secret had affected me, which I found really interesting because I know it has and I hate it. I asked them how they thought it had and they said, "You believe the secret is necessary on some levels and it exerts fear over you, manipulates you. You were taught this over a period of time, it's a form of brainwashing. Choice is removed from you." I know this is true and found it thought-provoking as I've worked with the children of a strict religious sect myself for many years, without considering myself to be in a similar situation; I'm now wondering if I've worked with these children partly in order to gain a deeper understanding into my own life. The connection now seems obvious but I honestly never made it until I got in touch with Coping.

I continued to think about whether sending off this letter was the right way forward for several weeks, coming to a different conclusion each day. So many thoughts went round in my head: what if all the terrible things that my father had prophesised happening actually happened? What if he found a way to harm my family? What if nothing came of it and I felt embarrassed? What if it's the best thing to do for my family and I? What if it helps end the secrecy surrounding priests' children? What on earth is the right thing to do?

In the end, something else overtook my attention for a few weeks, so I was spared making a decision for a little while.

Elizabeth, my wonderful therapist, said that she thought I'd suffered abuse in all this, because the signs that showed were similar to someone who'd suffered another more well-known type such as sexual abuse. I was shocked to hear this. I'd always wondered, at the back of my mind, whether my father was right; that there was nothing wrong with the situation, and that I should just shut up and deal with it and stop making trouble for everyone. But to hear someone say that I was showing signs of abuse was really eye-opening. It suddenly helped to take the guilt away – I'd always felt like the whole thing was my fault in some way –

because if someone else was causing the abuse then it wasn't my fault; it was their problem not mine. I asked her what signs I'd shown of this, and she said there were abandonment and rejection issues which may have arisen from being told not to talk about him or acknowledge anything to do with him, as well as from meetings with him in the past and what I've heard and read from and about him and others; this all constitutes a form of abuse and probably affected my self-esteem and contributed to me feeling worthless and having an "I'm not worth loving so who cares" kind of attitude that led me to take risks pre-accident. Her words resonated a lot with me and I knew there was much truth in it, and I found it refreshing to hear this new perspective. Together we came up with the idea that I might write about the experience with my father and the NDE; because it could be cathartic and healing. I liked this concept but initially felt apprehensive in case it was contravening some terrible hold the Catholic Church had over me. But when I got home that day I felt rage at the Church having such power over me, and started to write at once. I haven't stopped since; although saying that, my children will always be my first priority and finding time to write around looking after them is always logistically interesting, but not impossible.

At times I've stopped and asked myself why I'm writing this book. It is cathartic, and being able to present a more or less linear timeline does help to make sense of a lot of experiences. Perhaps as a result of being a forced secret I've always felt a need to be frank and honest (when I was younger a teacher declared me to be a bit too honest at times, perhaps she thought that some things are better left unsaid if they cause trouble; I think that this depends entirely on what is being left unsaid). Maybe being honest about my experiences feels like a counter to the deceit and the lies by omission that have always confused me. Pope Francis called the veil of secrecy drawn over children of priests, "one of the evils, one of the evils of the Church... a 'complicit' evil,"[50] and someone has to speak out about this "'complicit' evil". Coping International are doing it, and now so am I. I suspect that my NDE has helped me have the confidence to do this. Large organisations are good at hiding this sort of thing, the uncovering of the British establishment's paedophile ring by Operation Yewtree being a prime example. But this clericalism 'evil' or abuse must stop so that future children of priests (believe me there will be lots because priests are human!) are celebrated openly and not subjected to forced silence, and grow up in a situation where normal love from *both* parents is encouraged and expected.

While writing this book I came to the conclusion that the best way to proceed (initially) with the letter from Coping to the UK church official, the UN and the Vatican, was to leave myself and my father anonymous (to start with) but to tell my story in order to raise awareness and so that I could gauge their response and think about what to do next. A letter – keeping me anonymous – was sent off on 11th August 2015.

I am contacting you in my capacity as founder and chairperson of Coping International, an organisation dedicated to people who have been fathered by Catholic Priests... We have been contacted by an individual, who presently wishes to remain nameless and instead has trusted their documentation to Coping, so as to secure in writing, the preferred approach... Our client shall be named Alice... Her father is a Catholic Priest... It was made known to the diocese at an early stage, of Alice's mother's pregnancy and yet the reaction was certainly not child centred. Herein lays the onus of responsibility toward the... Diocese... Whilst, Alice's father holds responsibility toward her, that he was encouraged and defended in his self-centred decision, extrapolates an injunction that was silently created by clericalist tendencies, is nothing short of abhorrent. "It is in the circumstances impossible and inappropriate for there to be anything like an involved, normal father-daughter relationship." To make such a statement is to undermine the need within a child to know where he/she belongs placing the self-centred needs of the adult first. Of all the communica-

tions, of which are numerous, among them, one signed letter from a Cardinal, who states, "I thought it might help to have the professional opinion of someone who knows the parties involved." The 'someone' the Cardinal refers to is a Psychiatrist. In a letter written to Alice's mum, the Psychiatrist states "The Cardinal has written to me about the ongoing situation. [...] He is unhappy about the suggestion that [Alice's father] should leave the priesthood." Yet the Cardinal himself commented in his own signed document, "I continue to be very concerned for Alice's health and future well-being." Alice's mother in a further letter... some years later commented, "[...] I was not being listened to, and it was obvious to me, that he had been extracting himself [reference to Alice's natural birth father] out of any responsibility." That the Cardinal has left this situation untended to, still in a state of flux, is nothing short of astounding.

The communications are many... and paint a picture of subterfuge, illusion, deception, fear mongering, evasiveness and imposed secrecy. This child, now an adult, continues to attend regular psychotherapy sessions and will continue to do so for the foreseeable future having described the secrecy as "extreme". To hoist the onus onto her natural father is to largely shirk onus. The diocese shares equal responsibility as regards child neglect and emotional child abuse toward Alice, having participated and fortified efforts at stifling her natural development since her conception, her innate curiosities and putting in its place absence, enforced secrecy and a burdened mother. This sadly amounts to child neglect, itself defined in terms of abuse. This is child abuse, make no mistake... the diocese directly, not indirectly or 'absently' played a hand, consciously and in full knowledge...

The coordinator of Coping had included a thought here that had already begun growing in my mind; while my father's actions (in my opinion) are entirely his own responsibility, there was already a framework of cover-up and secrecy that existed around the children of priests in the Catholic Church, and it's this that's the overall problem because without it no priests would be able to arrange their own children's adoptions, get the mothers of their children to sign confidentiality agreements, distance themselves from their sons and daughters and refuse to meet them for years and years: "To hoist the onus onto her natural father is to largely shirk onus. The diocese shares equal responsibility as regards child neglect and emotional child abuse toward Alice, having participated and fortified efforts at stifling her natural development." There seems to be two issues present in many cases like mine: the personal choice of the father to distance himself and withdraw normal parental love (this is not always the case, as seen in the testimonies on the Coping International website, some priests maintain close, loving 'normal' parental relationships with their children, seeing them almost every day of their childhood and young adulthood) and the framework of secrecy that has clearly existed to hold up such cases for many years within the Catholic Church.

A couple of weeks later, the church official responded:

Thank you very much for your email… my experience has been that these matters have been handled sensitively and well, including trying to ensure that the priest has the means to support his child.

In your letter you refer to the contact that has been made to you by an unnamed individual and the circumstances appertaining to the birth of her child… While I respect your client's wish for anonymity, you will understand that on the basis of the information you have given, I am not in any position to either understand or comment on that particular matter.

As regards my meeting your client this I would gladly do but will necessarily require the disclosure of pertinent information on the part of your client.

Coping International wrote back, expressing my wishes that one of them accompany me to this meeting. The church official responded quickly:

Thank you very much indeed for your email. My Private Secretary...
will arrange an appointment through you.

However, I would like to emphasise that at some point I will be
seeking a time for a private conversation with this lady.

Both Coping International and I thought that the sentence,
"However, I would like to emphasise that at some point I will be
seeking a time for a private conversation with this lady" sounded
rather ominous. Why private? So as it stands at the moment, a
meeting will be arranged between the church official, myself and
Coping International at some point in the future. Interestingly,
when they heard I was writing this book, a member of my family
gave me another letter from the Cardinal who 'mediated'
between my parents in the 1990s. It's clearly the one that the letter
from my mother dated May 1998 is replying to. An extract from
it reads,

> *Dear Emma,*
> *... I know that you realise that I have to balance compassion and truth*
> *with justice... I feel quite annoyed that I was not told about what*
> *happened in 1977 by any of the parties concerned. I was at that time*
> *the Bishop of the Diocese and so ultimately responsible. Such a serious*
> *matter should have been referred to me. I would certainly not have*
> *proceeded with the ordination of J had I known what had taken place,*
> *and the consequences of it. The difficulties you and Hannah have met*
> *could have been avoided had the right decisions been taken... in 1977.*
> *The wrong decisions were taken. I do see how the presence and avail-*
> *ability of her father would have been important to Hannah in her*
> *formative years. It is not quite the same now that Hannah has reached*
> *adulthood.*

He goes on to say that he has to think of James' well-being and
that whatever took place in the past James has rights both as a
priest and a human being, and that he has to respect these. While

the Cardinal does not apologise, he admits that events in 1977 were handled badly by the Catholic Church, this is the first time I've read such an admission from anyone.

In July 2015, I re-watched one of the most wonderful NDE accounts I've ever heard of on YouTube because it always makes me feel happy and totally puts things into perspective. In 1991, Pam Reynolds had a near-death experience while under close medical scrutiny. A more perfectly monitored 'death' could hardly be imagined, after being diagnosed with a large aneurism close to the brain stem:

> Because of the difficult position of the aneurysm, Reynolds was predicted to have no chance of survival. As a last resort, Robert F. Spetzler – a neurosurgeon of the Barrow Neurological Institute in Phoenix, Arizona – decided that a rarely performed surgical procedure, known as hypothermic cardiac arrest, was necessary to improve Pam's outcome. During this procedure, also known as a standstill operation, Pam's body temperature was lowered to 50°F (10°C), her breathing and heartbeat stopped, and the blood drained from her head. Her eyes were closed with tape and small earplugs with speakers were placed in her ears. These speakers emitted audible clicks which were used to check the function of the brain stem to ensure that she had a flat EEG – or a non-responsive brain – before the operation proceeded.[51]

It was during this time of hypothermic cardiac arrest, when her brain was concluded to be completely unresponsive, that Pam had her near-death experience.

She felt she was pulled out of her body and floated above the operating room; later she was able to describe what was happening to her body and the instruments that were used as well as conversations between staff in detail that later shocked the medical staff including Dr Robert F. Spetzler. She felt herself being pulled towards a light and beings surrounded by light. She recognised her deceased grandmother, and communicated to her that she wasn't a perfect person and didn't feel worthy enough to be with all the beings of light. Her grandmother kindly explained that she, Pam, had been like a child sent away to school, and that they'd expected her to make mistakes. But it was how she cleaned them up that made those who watched over her proud.[52] I love that bit, it's so wise. We are all like children, sent here to learn, and we all make mistakes – in fact it's expected. But we all have a chance to learn from the mistakes and to repair things. Afterwards, taken aback by Pam's knowledge of what was going on in the operating room, when asked what he thought had really happened to Pam, Dr Robert F. Spetzler said he believes it to be: "The height of egotism to say that something can't happen just because we can't explain it."[53] Perhaps Dr Raymond Moody is right when he says that in the end NDEs won't be explained and accepted by a breakthrough in science, but ultimately by a breakthrough in logic.[54] His book, *Glimpses of Eternity*, discusses shared death experiences at the time of a loved one's death where one or more people in the room are drawn up into the dying person's experience of leaving their body, sometimes watching the dying person's life review with them. Perhaps these shared death phenomena could take us closer to this breakthrough in logic.

Compassion seems to be a key component for possibly having a shared death experience. In a different way it also seems key in Pam's experience – her grandmother showed great compassion for her, and in encouraging her to show it to herself. Compassion seems to be key in any kind of genuine love, and I slowly began to be able to apply it to both myself and my father. I realised that if I was going to really move on from the after-effects of the accident, I had to forgive myself for it. I manage to do this bit by bit each day and week; it would be fair to say it's a work in progress but I'm getting there and it's very healing.

In the same way, I know compassion towards James would be

healing for myself and my family, and that's coming on quite nicely. I do believe that if we act in a way that has negative conse-quences we're acting from "fear, pain and limited perspectives"[55] (I know I've acted like that before), and that the worse the action the more consumed with self-hatred, confusion and pain that individual must be; so that judging and condemning that individual reinforces their beliefs, and so the cycle goes on. If I set out to name and shame my father I'd be acting out of hate instead of love, and the negative effects of that may reverberate down to my own children and the pattern may continue. What I actually want to do (and hope I am doing) is treat him with compassion, which is not the same as condoning anything. I just think that's the only way we will all fully heal. We need to try and end the negativity to move forwards.

I've come to the firm conclusion that any type of witch-hunt – that exposes the identity of any priest who has fathered a child – would be as destructive as any actions taken by those priests and the Church. We can't change the past, but we can change the future, and the structure of the Catholic Church ultimately needs to transform, because enforced secrecy is not healthy for the children of priests. I suppose this is really what I want to say: my father is not a bad person, we have had some civilised conversations and he often sent money while I was growing up. It is my choice that my children and I don't see him, because I feel that until there is complete honesty and love any meetings seem to inspire negative rather than positive thoughts and outcomes. It is a confusing situation, often not clear-cut. But what is clear to me, in my case and in many other cases around the world: in separating from and silencing their children, priests are trying to adhere to the doctrine of the Church that they've become part of (whilst perhaps hiding behind this doctrine because they don't want to be parents), but what if the doctrine, in this instance, is wrong?

I think that the structure of the Catholic Church needs to change, because as I've previously discussed enforced secrecy is not healthy for the children of priests. We've got into a pattern, a habit, of thinking that Catholic priests must be celibate because "the obligation to be celibate is seen as a consequence of the obligation to observe *perfect and perpetual* continence for the sake of the Kingdom of heaven". Advocates see clerical celibacy as "a special gift of God by which sacred ministers can more easily remain close to Christ with an undivided heart, and can dedicate themselves more freely to the service of God and their neighbour".[56] But aside from the fact that this clerical celibacy clearly isn't working, it's also inconsistent: sometimes exceptions are made for individuals or whole categories of people, for example married Protestant clergymen are allowed to convert to Catholicism. In my opinion, the inconsistencies of the application of celibacy make it more or less nonsensical. A constructive way forward seems to be for the Catholic Church to evolve into an institution where priests are not put in a position where they are judged to lack the 'discipline' of celibacy if and when they father children, but to make celibacy optional, making the Church one where their children are celebrated as miracles who are treated with love and compassion. Then the Church becomes one where, as the Vatican states on its website, it "calls together" people in "unity",[57] rather than dividing them and hiding children away in shame. This may sound impossible, but it's not, it just requires a shift in perspective. It's nice to know that "In the other realm... our physical limitations become clear to us, so we're able to understand why we did things and we feel only compassion... In the other realm, we're all one. We're all the same."[58] I suspect that we're here to understand how to feel this compassion from the inside out, while having the illusion that we're separate from everybody else.

While writing this book, I've realised that what I'd really like to see happen is a public discussion developing (hopefully with the emphasis on constructive help rather than destructive divisiveness) about priests' children. Let's look at the bigger picture – is this pattern of secrecy and silencing sustainable for the foreseeable future? For how many more decades? Catholic priests having children is a distasteful topic to many; I understand that. It goes against so many traditions and beliefs. However, we have to accept that it is happening and will continue to happen, for the sake of the children involved (and their fathers). How can we turn it into a positive experience for all involved? How can priests be priests, yet also be good fathers, and by this I mean seeing their children a huge amount from birth onwards, loving them, creating a normal father-child relationship? If it's impossible, how come so many other religious leaders manage to do it very successfully? Perhaps George Bernard Shaw's words would be appropriate here: "Progress is impossible without change, and those who cannot change their minds cannot change anything."

Final Thoughts

Happily, I'm now at the point where I can look back and see how utterly transformed my life has become since 31st January 1998. I can marvel at this in wonder and awe, because I was given another chance to come back and live my life again, learning how to replace the lack of love and hurt that I'd unwittingly chosen to internalise and let run my life, with love and compassion for both myself and others. Before January 1998 there's no way I could have imagined that I'd be a mother, writer, teacher, and that I'd have an unshakeable faith in life beyond our life on earth. Don't get me wrong, there are a normal amount of good and bad days in my life, but I now know that these annoying bits are just as much why we're here as the brilliant bits (and there are *infinite* brilliant bits – the three main ones being my funny, quirky, beautiful, utterly amazing children who I love absolutely unconditionally), they are helping us become who we are meant to be.

I now see that all the different parts of my life make sense and are becoming integrated, although I think this will probably always be a work in progress. And I'm enjoying being able to integrate spirituality into being the child of a priest! (I set up a Facebook page called "spiritualjourneysndes" and I love connecting with people via it who have similar views.) Elizabeth pointed out that we all have our shadow sides, and I think that accepting the whole of ourselves, the dark and the light, and accepting the same in each other, is one of the most realistic, healing ways forward. My own experiences have shown me that we can experience what feels like excellent physical and mental health in our lives on earth as well as acute physical and mental illness and distress. The two opposing states do not define who we are; they are manifestations of *how* we are, especially how we are feeling about ourselves.

One of the most important things I've learned in all this, something I hope my children come to understand much earlier

than I did, is that you are absolutely in charge of your own des
You can create your own universe around yourself, of cou
within certain unchangeable limits in your environment, but it's
amazing what can be changed if love and kindness are at the root
of your actions; either love and kindness towards yourself or others
or, even better, both. Other people's opinions and 'truths' about you
don't define you unless you let them.

I know it could be argued that I'm delusional because I've
described something that has been coined a 'near-death
experience', because I understand that many people just aren't
comfortable with the idea that we are essentially spiritual, that
consciousness is not just inside our heads, that we are capable of
having very real experiences away from our bodies, giving rise
to the notion that there is life beyond life on earth and all the
implications that that brings. I can totally relate to that point of
view because I shared it before my accident. All I can say is that
everything I've written about in this book is completely true; the
only things I've changed are some of the names, a couple of
dates, and I've left out some of the more gory details
surrounding the accident. I'm also aware that it could be argued
that because I was not in a good way before the accident, having
been out all night drinking, having led a hedonistic lifestyle, that
my account of what happened next, i.e. the NDE, is not reliable.
All I can say is that I'm not drunk or tired now and can tell the
difference between reality and delusion; and I can relate every
other aspect of what happened that day with accurate detail.
During the NDE I did not feel the same as I did before or after it,
I had a heightened awareness of everything and felt fantastic.
Feelings/thoughts during that time went beyond ones normally
restrained by human bodily conditions. It was very real and
since it happened my life has totally transformed.

One of the most important things I've learned is that how you
feel about yourself, how you let yourself feel about other people's
actions that affect you, shapes your life. This is quite a refreshing

realisation because it puts you in the driver's seat. I'd let my life spiral down to near death because I couldn't get past the pain I'd internalised, and this was a choice I'd made, without consciously realising it. After the NDE, when I had a new perspective on life that put love for myself and others in absolute core position of importance, my life transformed. So even if someone is intentionally or unintentionally inflicting pain on you, you can still choose to love yourself and choose the best life on offer. Anybody perpetrating the pain will have to deal with their actions at some point; hence the life review. They are not your concern, you are. You can go back through your life and choose to view yourself with compassion, especially during the hardest times. Congratulate yourself for getting through those times, realise your strengths, your amazingness. Understand how you talk to yourself in your head; if it's negative, work out why. Imagine you love yourself then make all decisions based on that and see your life change.

So, why did all this happen to me? I experienced internalising the anti-love by my father and the Church, and I experienced real love away from my body when I was close to death. One was destructive, the other healing and inspiring. I felt what it's like to allow yourself to be destroyed through lies, secrecy and deceit, and I also felt what it's like to be fully alive, away from the human body in peace and love. I have been on a journey from that point on. I now know that I am always surrounded by love even if I'm having a bad day. Through Coping International I now know I am just one of many that this has happened to; there are hundreds, probably thousands of children around the world who have been fathered by Catholic priests and who've been shamed into silence, distanced from their fathers, in the name of God. When I nearly died and left my body, I was not asked to hide my identity and pretend I didn't exist. Real, unconditional love, which we all are and are capable of showing, does not include secrecy, deceit, lies and false prophets. If I'd gone further into the spiritual realm, and one day we will all do this, I now know from NDE accounts that I would have had a life review, met people I've known who've died, and have been continuously surrounded by this infinite love.

That love really is the most important thing is a truth as old as time itself. Near-death experiences are providing first-hand accounts of this love and how and why it's important. The strongest force on this earth that has helped me carry on through the most difficult times is the love of my mother. She constantly fought for more recognition and normality in a weird situation, feeling conflicted most of the time but always doing what she thought was best. We have become so close since the accident; I think the truth is that when there's just been the two of you (until I had my own utterly amazing family) and you've both nearly died in dramatic fashions, you understand what really matters.

One of the most common elements of a deeper NDE is that the person is asked a question by the being of light that they meet. This question, while often hard to define, generally means, "Have you learned to love yourself and others?" All NDE survivors who've experienced this agree that love is the most important thing of all, here and after, and that love and knowledge are the two things we can take with us after we die. Many say they realise that money, status, possessions, wealth etc. are not the things to be focussing on. They come back with a new appreciation of their friends, family, nature and the environment, and are happy to lead simpler lives. From my point of view, although I did not meet a Being of Light (I wish I had!) I found myself changed after the experience of being wrapped in love and light and being shown who I am without all the fear and lack of self-worth. Even though I wasn't explicitly shown or told that love is the most important thing, I came back with a sense that it is and my life has changed around this. And even though I wasn't explicitly told how important knowledge is, I came back with a crazy desire to learn. Incidentally, given that my experience involved and centred on a loving light, Dr Moody writes:

Many of my fellow researchers feel it is the encounter with the mystical light that leads to positive changes in the personalities of those who have a near-death experience. The research of Dr Morse bears this out. He examined the effects of the various elements of a near-death experience... on those who have had them. He concluded that spiritual encounters with light are the element most profoundly linked with positive transformation.[59]

Since I didn't speak to anyone or any being directly during the NDE I wonder whether this gives the best clue as to why I and my life transformed so much after it.

Love and compassion being at the root of all that is important in life is a truth that's been documented throughout the centuries by people of all nations, colours and creeds. In the Bible, 1 Corinthians 13:13 reads, "And now these three remain, faith, hope and love. And the greatest of these is love." Colossians 3:14 reads, "And over all these virtues put on love, which binds them all together in perfect unity." Gautama Buddha said, "You can search throughout the entire universe for someone who is more deserving of your love and affection than you are yourself, and that person is not to be found anywhere. You, yourself, as much as anybody in the entire universe, deserve your love and affection," and also, "If you truly loved yourself, you could never hurt another." Adam Pascal, atheist, said, "We are all given a gift of existence and of being sentient beings, and I think true happiness lies in love and compassion."[60] Teresa MacBain, pastor turned atheist, said "for me the meaning of life, or the meaning in life, is helping people and loving people."[61] Oscar Wilde said, "Keep love in your heart. A life without it is like a sunless garden when the flowers are dead." Lao Tzu said, "Being deeply loved by someone gives you strength, while loving someone deeply gives you courage." Mother Teresa said, "Spread love everywhere you go. Let no one ever come to you without leaving happier," and also, "I have found the paradox, that if you love until it hurts, there can be no more hurt, only more love." Lord Rama, Hindu lord of virtue, said, "I laugh, I love, I hope, I try, I hurt, I need, I fear, I cry. And I know you do the same things too. So we're really not that different, me and you." Plato said, "Love is the pursuit of the whole." NDE survivor Dannion Brinkley said, "I believe that the only way to create love is to consciously *be* love."[62] Carl Sagan said, "For small creatures such as we, the vastness is only bearable through love." Anita Moorjani said, "Unconditional love is our birth right, not judgement or condemnation, and there's nothing we need to do to earn it. This is simply who and what we are." Carlos Barrios, Mayan Elder and Ajq'ij of the Eagle Clan, said, "The greatest wisdom is in simplicity. Love, respect, tolerance, sharing, gratitude, forgiveness. It's not complex or elaborate. The real knowledge is free. It's encoded in your DNA. All you need is within you. Great teachers have said that from the beginning. Find your heart and you will find your way." Nancy Rynes, NDE survivor, said, "In choosing to love, we choose to open ourselves to learning and living our lives fully as spiritual expressions."[63] By listing these quotes, I'm hoping to share my belief that pretty much all of us, from all backgrounds, cultures, countries and creeds ultimately believe in the same power: love. It's the most emotionally, spiritually and psychologically healing power there is; one that transcends human belief systems and ultimately unites us all as one. With this in mind, the conflict, exclusivity, separation, judgement and divisiveness that exist in our world makes no sense. But maybe living in a conflicted world is all part of continuing to find out who on earth we are. It might be worth bearing in mind that, "Spirit asks that we put aside our differences and figure out some ways to cherish and respect each other as the spiritual creations we are. It doesn't mean we have to agree with everyone, but it does mean that through love and compassion, we work to overcome our differences and solve our problems, together, as one humanity."[64] Compassion heals, and it makes the world more beautiful.

Understanding that life goes on after we 'die' sheds a new perspective on everything that happens. I now know I'm loved both down here and up there, and I have lots of love to give my own family and friends. One of my aims, since realising I had a near-death experience and understanding the mind-blowing implications of this, has been to comprehend what would have happened if I'd gone further into the experience. Anita Moorjani says that during her NDE she saw that we are all love, at our core. While enveloped in a sea of love and acceptance, she was:

> able to look at myself with fresh eyes, and I saw that I was a beautiful being of the universe. I understood that just the fact that I existed made me worthy of... tender regard rather than judgement. I didn't need to do anything specific; I deserved to be loved simply because I existed, nothing more and nothing less... I'm loved unconditionally, for no other reason than simply because I exist. I was transformed in unimaginable clarity as I realised that this expanded, magnificent essence was really me. It was the truth of my being.[65]

Following this train of thought, my father is also made from love. We are all on earth with the free will to make decisions about our lives and he has made his decisions because he felt them to be right at the time. He has reassured me in letters that members of his congregation find him useful and helpful. I'm genuinely glad he has been of help to others. Maybe it was confusing for him, being encouraged by a more senior priest to lead a life of secrecy, to give up his free will and obey church doctrine at the price of rejecting his child, maybe that hasn't all panned out as he thought it would, who knows. With the knowledge that we all have a life review at the end of our lives (on earth), I don't feel in a position to judge him or anyone else for their actions because we'll all end up taking responsibility for the things we have done in the end anyway, most definitely me included. I sometimes wonder whether after we die and fully accept ourselves and actions, my father and I will be able to be closer. I kind of suspect we will.

Acknowledgements

There are so many utterly amazing people who I want to thank. Firstly, my strong and courageous mother, who has stood by me through thick and thin – providing so much love, and my husband and children for generally being their wonderful selves and for making me laugh a lot and for also providing masses of love; laughing is one of my favourite things to do, so please keep it up! The team at O-Books and John Hunt for giving me this invaluable opportunity to share my story, and for patiently working with me and answering my random questions. Each and every one of my exquisitely amazing friends from past and present – you know who you are! – for always being there and for giving me some of the best and most memorable times of my life. My wonderful cousins, aunts and uncles, parents-and-brothers-in-law, for the many great times. Ursula, for all the fabulous conversations, understanding and love. The doctors and nurses who saved my life and looked after me, both in Tenerife and England – words can't describe the level of gratitude I feel. Dr Penny Sartori, for her invaluable insights and support, Elizabeth for helping me turn my life around – I strongly suspect you may be an earth angel! The co-ordinator and founder of Coping International, who changed my life and is currently changing the lives of many other people. The academics, psychotherapists and near-death survivors from around the globe who have already responded with great warmth and compassion after hearing about this book. To all of you, I'm truly grateful.

Endnotes

Chapter One

1. Barry, C. (2015) "Shrouded In Secrecy", the *Irish Catholic* (Online). Available at: http://irishcatholic.ie/article/shrouded-secrecy

2. Moorjani, A. (2014) Q & A with Anita, Anita Moorjani: Remember Your Magnificence (Online). Available at: http://www.anitamoorjani.com/qa-with-anita-17th-october-2014/

3. Keenan, Marie, Child Sexual Abuse and the Catholic Church: Gender, Power, and Organizational Culture, OUP USA, 2011, pp 42–43

4. *Child First Document*, 2.3.1, IV & VI, Available at: http://www.dcya.gov.ie/documents/Publications/ChildrenFirst.pdf

5. Keenan, pp 42–43

6. Barry, C. (2015) "Shrouded In Secrecy", the *Irish Catholic* (Online). Available at: http://irishcatholic.ie/article/shrouded-secrecy

7. Dobbs, D. (2011) "Teenage Brains", *National Geographic* (Online). Available at: http://ngm.nationalgeographic.com/2011/10/teenage-brains/dobbs-text

8. Andrews, A. (2007) "Madchester, Spice, rave and grunge", *BBC News* (Online). Available at: http://news.bbc.co.uk/1/hi/magazine/6767179.stm

9. Barry, C. (2015) "Shrouded In Secrecy", the *Irish Catholic* (Online). Available at: http://irishcatholic.ie/article/shrouded-secrecy

10. Handler, S. MEd (2013) "5 Reasons Why Keeping Family Secrets Could Be Harmful", Psych Central (Online). Available at: http://psychcentral.com/blog/archives/2013/08/22/5-reasons-why-keeping-family-secrets-could-be-harmful/

11. Black, C. MSW, PhD (2006) "Understanding the Pain of Abandonment", *Psychology Today* (Online). Available at: https://www.psychologytoday.com/blog/the-many-faces-addiction/201006/understanding-the-pain-abandonment

12. "Playa de las Américas – Tenerife, Visit Tenerife" (Online). Available at: http://www.spain-tenerife.com/UK/americas.html

Chapter Three

13. Jack, "10 Tips to Understanding the Weather on Tenerife", The Real Tenerife (Online). Available at: http://therealtenerife.com/posts/10-tips-to-understanding-the-weather-on-tenerife/

Chapter Four

14. Holbrook, Troy L. PhD; Anderson, John P. PhD; Sieber, William J. PhD; Browner, Dierdre MPH; Hoyt, David B. MD, FACS (1999) "Outcome After Major Trauma", *The Journal of Trauma and Acute Care Surgery* (Online). Available at: http://journals.lww.com/jtrauma/Abstract/1999/05000/Outcome_after_Major_Trauma__12_Month_and_18_Month.3.aspx

15. Brach, T., "The Power of Radical Acceptance: Healing Trauma through the Integration of Buddhist Meditation and Psychotherapy", Tara Brach: Meditation, Emotional Healing, Spiritual Awakening (Online). Available at: http://www.tarabrach.com/articles/trauma.html

16. Hunniford, G. (2015) "White feathers that convince Gloria Hunniford guardian angels do exist..." Daily Mail (Online). Available at: http://www.dailymail.co.uk/news/article-2771542/White-feathers-convince-Gloria-Hunniford-guardian-angels-DO-exist-make-certain-darling-daughter-Caron-Keating-watching-her.html

17. Ibid

Chapter Five

18. Gholipour, B. (2014) "New Technique Helps Find Hidden

Consciousness in Coma Patients", Live Science (Online). Available at: http://www.livescience.com/48317-hidden-awareness-in-coma-vegetative-state.html

19. Williams, K., "Dr. George Ritchie's Near-Death Experience", Near Death (Online). Available at: http://www.near-death.com/experiences/notable/george-ritchie.html#a01

20. "Raymond Moody", Wikipedia (Online). Available at: https://en.wikipedia.org/wiki/Raymond_Moody

21. Williams, K., "Dr Raymond Moody's Near-Death Experience Research", Near Death (Online). Available at: http://www.near-death.com/science/experts/raymond-moody.html

22. "Raymond Moody", Wikipedia (Online). Available at: https://en.wikipedia.org/wiki/Raymond_Moody

23. Moody, R., *The Light Beyond*, Rider, New Edition, 2005, pp 100–101

24. Ibid pp 154–165

25. Ibid pp 41–42

26. Ibid p 102

27. Moorjani, A., *Dying To Be Me: My Journey from Cancer, to Near Death, to True Healing*, Hay House, 2012, p 61

28. Ibid pp 62–63

29. Ibid pp 64–65

30. Ibid pp 65–66

31. Ibid pp 68–69

32. Ibid p 69

33. Ibid p 89

34. Ibid pp 100–101

35. Ibid p 70

36. Ibid p 186

37. Ibid p 185

38. Sartori, P., *The Wisdom of Near-Death Experiences*, Watkins Publishing Ltd, 2014, pp 190–191

39. Moody, R., *Reflections on Life After Life*, Kindle, 2011, p 265

40. Brinkley, D., Perry, P., *Saved by the Light*, Piatkus, 2011, p 144

41. Hamilton, D., *It's The Thought That Counts*, Hay House UK, 2008, p 90
42. Van Lommel, P., *Consciousness Beyond Life: The Science of the Near-Death Experience*, HarperOne, 2011, p 237
43. Popova, M., "Carl Sagan on Science and Spirituality", Brain Pickings (Online). Available at: http://www.brainpickings.org/2013/06/12/carl-sagan-on-science-and-spirituality/
44. Moody, R., *Paranormal: My Life in Pursuit of the Afterlife*, Kindle, 2013, pp 127–128
45. Moorjani, A., pp 154–155
46. Moorjani, A. (2013) Facebook (Online). Available at: https://www.facebook.com/Anita.Moorjani/posts/552809124764090
47. "Mental Health and Well Being", Coping International (Online). Available at: http://www.copinginternational.com/mental-health-well/
48. Ibid
49. Ibid
50. Pope Francis, "Address of Pope Francis to Members of the 'Corallo' Association," Clementine Hall (2014) (Online). Available at: http://mobile.vatican.va/content/francescomobile/en/speeches/2014/march/documents/papa-francesco_20140322_associazione-corallo.html
51. "Pam Reynolds case", Wikipedia (Online). Available at: https://en.wikipedia.org/wiki/Pam_Reynolds_case
52. https://www.youtube.com/watch?v=Bu1ErDeQ0Zw
53. Ibid
54. Moody, *Paranormal: My Life in Pursuit of the Afterlife*
55. Moorjani, A., p 170
56. "Clerical celibacy (Catholic Church)", Wikipedia (Online). Available at: https://en.wikipedia.org/wiki/Clerical_celibacy_(Catholic_Church)
57. "Catechism of the Catholic Church", Vatican (Online). Available at: http://www.vatican.va/archive/ccc_css/archive/cat

echism/p123a9p1.htm

58. Moorjani, A., p 170

Final Thoughts

59. Moody, R., *Glimpses of Eternity*, Rider, 2011, p 83
60. Tarico, V. (2014) "20 amazing quotes from atheists that prove religion isn't necessary for a meaningful life", *Salon* (Online). Available at: http://www.salon.com/2014/02/11/20_amazing_ quotes_from_atheists_that_prove_religion_isnt_necessary_for _a_meaningful_life_partner/
61. Ibid
62. Brinkley, D., Perry, P., p 105
63. Rynes, N., *Awakenings from the Light*, Kindle, 2015, p 50
64. Rynes, N., p 53
65. Moorjani, A., pp 69–70

Note To Reader

Thank you so much for purchasing *Dying to Be Free*. My sincere hope is that you derived as much from reading this book as I hoped for in creating it. If you have a few moments, please feel free to add your review of the book at your favourite online site for feedback (Amazon, Apple iTunes Store, Goodreads etc). Also, if you would like to connect with other books that I have coming in the near future, please visit my website for news on upcoming works and other information:

https://www.facebook.com/spiritualjourneysNDEs

or www.hannahrobinson.webs.com or contact me directly at hannahrobinson007@outlook.com.

Warmest regards,

Hannah Robinson

BOOKS

O is a symbol of the world, of oneness and unity; this eye represents knowledge and insight. We publish titles on general spirituality and living a spiritual life. We aim to inform and help you on your own journey in this life.

Visit our website: http://www.o-books.com

Find us on Facebook:
https://www.facebook.com/OBooks

Follow us on Twitter: @obooks